122

Sexual Style

Robert Meyners
and Claire Wooster

SEXUAL STYLE

Facing and Making Choices about Sex

New York and London
Harcourt Brace Jovanovich

Requests for permission to make copies
of any part of the work should be mailed to:
Permissions, Harcourt Brace Jovanovich, Inc.
757 Third Avenue, New York, N.Y. 10017

The authors wish to thank Pantheon Books,
a Division of Random House, Inc.,
for permission to quote from KNOTS, by R. D. Laing.
Copyright © 1970 by The R. D. Laing Trust.

Printed in the United States of America

Library of Congress Cataloging in Publication Data

Meyners, Robert, 1922–
Sexual style.

Bibliography: p.
1. Sex. Customs.   2. Choice (Psychology)
I. Wooster, Claire, 1942–   joint author.
II. Title.
HQ12.M48   301.41'7   78–22266
ISBN 0–15–181399–X

First edition

B C D E

Contents

Sexual Style

Introduction:
Is There a Better Way?

A bed is no doubt a popular place for sex because it is pleasant and comfortable. A Procrustean bed, however, is another matter. Procrustes was a character in Greek legend who put his guests in a special bed. If they were too short for the bed, he would stretch them till they fit; if they were too tall, he chopped off their legs. He never offered a different bed. From time immemorial the sexual bed has been like Procrustes'. The bodies and minds of generations of lovers have been bent out of shape to make them conform to a sexual mode that does not fit.

Today we have a freedom to choose our ways of being sexual that was generally unavailable in the past. But a strange thing has happened. Conformity has been replaced, not by freedom, but by confusion:

"I've always been pretty active sexually, but sometimes I feel bad about it . . . guilty or something."

"I like to have sex the 'old-fashioned way,' but my lover is always wanting to do something freaky."

"Sex is okay for me, but sometimes I wonder if I'm missing a lot. There's no fireworks or anything."

"At my age, everyone seems to think I should climb up on a shelf. I begin to feel guilty when I get horny."

"When I was single, I was expected to be 'good,' and I was, believe me. Then one day I got married and suddenly I was supposed to be hot as a firecracker in bed. There's got to be a better way!"

These are the words of people bewildered by sexual choices. No doubt each of them feels there must be a better way. Where once we were forced to fit the bed Procrustes gave us, now we're forced to choose from a multitude of beds. If you have ever wondered whether there is a better way for you personally, this book is for you.

With so many options available, however, you may ask if intelligent and satisfying choices can even be made. We believe the answer is a resounding yes. You do not have to grasp frantically at old, worn-out rules that serve no useful purpose. Neither do you have to stumble blindly into some sexual revolution of which you are the victim rather than the beneficiary. The strategies provided in the pages that follow provide a method of exploring your sexual values and determining what you wish them to be. These choices add up to what we call your sexual style.

This book does not recommend any particular sexual style. It does not argue for one set of values or one way of living.[1] Instead, it outlines choices and suggests possibilities. It invites you to identify and clarify *your own* sexual style. What do *you* want? What do *you* cherish? How do *you* usually act, feel, think? What would *you* like to change?

You will not be interested in all the options we present. You may even be appalled at some, such as anal sex or separating sex from love. Be assured: it's all right to feel disgust. This book is about recognizing your feelings and aligning them with your beliefs and behavior. Therefore, don't take offense—take hope! The fact that you have opinions means that you are that much closer to identifying your own sexual style.

We, too, have opinions and do not agree with every style we present. Nevertheless, each style we discuss is a serious alternative for some people. No scientific research has yet shown that one style is best for everyone; therefore, we have tried to be unbiased in sorting out the sexual alternatives people face. Because objectivity is always more an ideal than a reality, we have included a statement of our personal sexual values in the Epilogue. Our values are presented not to influence yours but to increase your chances of overcoming our biases. We respect your freedom.

This book is designed for unhurried reflection. Read a little . . . mull it over . . . try out a strategy . . . work *and play* with the material presented. Many of the exercises are not only more fun but also more rewarding if done with a close friend or a sexual partner.

We wish you well on a journey that has been a great and fulfilling adventure for many people. Your sexuality is a wondrous possession, a miraculous part of your being. In the exploration of its meaning, a measure of your whole existence may be splendidly revealed.

1

The Magic
in Your Mirror

Chances are you have had an experience like this: You are sitting in a waiting room with nothing to do but leaf aimlessly through magazines. You pick up one that pictures the latest fashions in clothes. To one style you react, "Yuk! I wouldn't paint the kitchen wearing that." To another, "That looks great, but I could never wear it. It's just not me." Or to another, "Hmmm, not bad. I wonder how I would feel in that."

Sexual style is like that. Some styles look good to you; others don't. Some are fine for someone else but don't fit who you really are. But there is a difference. You cannot change your sexual style as you do your clothes. Something far more fundamental is at stake in the choices you make, in the experimenting you do. Unlike clothing, your sexuality *is* skin-deep, even bone-deep.

In these first chapters we will look at your sexual style. What is sexual style? What are the main elements that form a sexual style? What is your sexual style? Later we can look at the details of your mode of being sexual, but for now we will take a quick overview, more like a few minutes in front of the mirror than a careful self-study.

Five Ticklish Questions

Sexual style arises out of the attitudes and beliefs you hold about sex and the way you carry these out in everyday life. It is reflected in the statements you are willing to make publicly, such as, "I am married [unmarried]." But a large part of sexual style remains hidden from other people. You do not go to a tea party and announce how many times a week you have an orgasm. There may even be a part of your sexual style you hide from yourself.

Many of the things you do result from the influence of models all around you. For example, you learned table manners by watching and listening to your parents. Not so with sex. It is impossible to develop a satisfying sexual style simply from the example of those around you. Too much is hidden. Even when children accidentally glimpse adults in sexual intercourse, they do not get much of an idea about how to manage it.

Instead, you develop sexual style by collecting bits and pieces of information and experience, fashioning these into a fabric, well or poorly suited to your needs. If you examine these choices carefully, they turn out to involve five basic questions. These are the ticklish questions we all face, either consciously or unconsciously, when choosing how we are to live sexually. If you ponder each question for yourself as you read along, you will bring into focus an image of your own sexual style. Your answers to some questions may be quite obvious to you. Others may be perplexing. Note these perplexities carefully. The sooner you begin to isolate the specific issues that need clarifying, the more helpful the ensuing pages will be.

1. *How important is sex in my life?* Is sex a sometime thing for you, or is it a rather central concern in your life? In an *expressive* sexual style, sex is an important and central concern, high on the list of life's priorities. In a *nonexpressive* style, sex has only minor significance in the total life-style.

Here are some *nonexpressive* views:

- "Sex? I can take it or leave it."

- "If an enticing person works on me, I may go along, but usually I'm not much into sex."

- "Passion is for kids. Sex can all too easily disrupt things that really matter."

These are some *expressive* views:

- "I really do enjoy sex!"

- "Sex takes a lot of my time and energy, and that's the way I like it. I don't let my job or friends interfere."

- "I'm miserable to be around if my sex life gets frustrated."

Which of these views most nearly reflects yours?

2. *Do I separate sex and love?* You may feel that sex is purely a physical matter, producing pleasure. Or you may feel that sex is also a deeply meaningful form of intimate communication between two people. In a *casual* sexual style, the personal relationship between the two people is unimportant or nonexistent. In a *relational* style, sex is regarded as less rewarding or morally wrong if it is not based on a loving relationship.

Here are some *casual* views:

- "I like sex without the complication of continuing a relationship."
- "If I am physically attracted to a person, and vice versa, there is no reason why we shouldn't enjoy each other sexually."
- "I can't see any reason to limit sex to love or intimacy."

These are some *relational* statements:

- "Sex without affection is messy and disappointing."
- "The better my relationship to my lover becomes, the better our sexual relationship is."
- "Sex is a deeply personal way of communicating my love."

How about you? Which of these statements most nearly reflects your feelings?

3. *Do I limit myself to one sexual partner?* You may feel that a variety of partners is desirable and permissible, or you may feel that one, and only one, sexual partner is appropriate at one time or even over a lifetime. In an *exclusive* sexual style, fidelity to one partner is the rule. In a *nonexclusive* style, no such limitation is made.

Here are some *nonexclusive* views:

- "I need variety in my sexual experience or else I get bored."
- "It is unrealistic to expect any one person to fulfill all my sexual needs."
- "I can love one person deeply and still enjoy other, more casual, sexual contacts."

These are some *exclusive* views:

- "Sexual fidelity is one of the most beautiful and precious gifts I can give to the one I love."
- "Sex can take on its full meaning only if it is reserved for the one person with whom I am in a committed relationship."
- "Sleeping around is just too much hassle. It's far more comfortable for me to keep things simple with one person."

How do you feel about this? Which of these ways fits you?

4. *What about children?* Your sexual style is *procreative* if you believe that the birth of children is the primary purpose of sex and the crowning joy of sexual experience. If you believe that children may be forgone without important loss to your life's satisfaction, then your style is *non-procreative*.

Here are some *nonprocreative* views:

- "Contraception is a marvelous boon to sexual pleasure."
- "In these days of worry about overpopulation, it is essential to separate sex from procreation."
- "I am not cut out to be a parent, but what nonsense that I should deny myself the pleasure of sex."
- "I may or may not have kids, but I'm *not* going to organize my sex life around children."

These are some *procreative* views:

- "The primary purpose of sex is, and will continue to be, the creation of new human life."
- "Certainly sex is pleasurable, but it is distorted when its reproductive purpose is denied."
- "My life could never be complete without children. They are my greatest joy."

Which of these views best reflects your own?

These four questions are simplifications of quite complicated issues. In each case, the black and the white are presented, not the subtle shades of gray in between. The subtleties we will explore later. For now, check your style in the spaces below. Mark the space you fit into when answering each question. If you are unclear where you fit, check the space marked "Unclear." Take note of these uncertainties. You will want to ponder these questions further.

Expressive	_____
Nonexpressive	_____
Unclear	_____

Casual	_____
Relational	_____
Unclear	_____

Exclusive	_____
Nonexclusive	_____
Unclear	_____
Procreative	_____
Nonprocreative	_____
Unclear	_____

There is one more ticklish question:

5. *What do I really want in a sexual partner?* One man may want an attractive, nonsmoking blond in her late twenties who is of Scandinavian descent, is a practicing Lutheran, plays the dulcimer, is intellectually stimulating, will pursue a career and still cook dinner. (A woman may want a man like that, too!) If that sounds to you like an unrealistic search for a perfect mate, you are probably right. But every person has some kind of list of qualifications for a sexual partner. Almost everyone has a decided preference for one gender or the other. You probably have ideas about how old your partner should be, about his or her race and religion, and many other characteristics.

The search for a permanent partner naturally involves some detailed (and even rigid) requirements. The expectations for more casual sexual contacts may be fewer and less precise. The man looking for his Scandinavian bride may not even think about the musical or culinary abilities of an attractive prospect for a one-night stand. Thus, there may be two sets of criteria: "He would be great for a wild affair, but I wouldn't marry a guy like that." Or, "We had a terrific time in bed, but she's not the sort of woman I want to marry."

Are you aware of your preferences in choosing a sexual partner? Here is a list of items that you might consider. Specify what, if any, requirements you have in each area.

	FOR A DATE	FOR A SPOUSE
Sex:		
Age:		
Physical appearance:		

	FOR A DATE	FOR A SPOUSE
Ethnic background:		
Religion:		
Social status:		
Job:		
Education:		
Personal habits:		
Sexual style:		
Other:		

Surely, not all of the requirements are of equal importance to you. To see which are really essential, try writing an advertisement of twenty-five words or less, like the ones you may have seen in the personal columns of magazines. You know the type: "Bachelor age 30 seeks . . ." "Fun-loving career girl looking for . . ." Would your specifications change if you were considering marriage? If so, what would they then be?

Often we are not aware of the choices we have made, let alone the reasons for these choices. The values we bring to bear on sexual decisions do not spring into our heads from nowhere. They come from the ideas, attitudes, and beliefs we have formed in experience over the years. They are influenced by parents, teachers, friends, childhood idols. Some attitudes we absorb from our culture like the air we breathe.

Families, schools, churches, the media, all tend to reinforce the same messages. When you considered the five questions, did you have any doubt what you *ought* to answer? Very likely not. We all "know" that sex is a good thing but that you can have too much of it. We all "know" that we "ought" to marry for life and be "faithful" to one partner and that it is certainly the "right" thing to have children. These are the cultural expectations most of us have carried around: be slightly expressive, relational, exclusive, and procreative! If you chose answers different from these, you had to overcome the influence of these traditional answers.

We can reexamine old attitudes, beliefs, and behaviors. We can look at their origins and decide whether they still make sense in the light of our current desires and aspirations. We do not have to pursue self-defeating behaviors. Even if you decide to follow the traditional patterns, examining your attitudes and actions alongside alternatives will reassure you that you have indeed made the right choices.

Looking Back in Wonder

The first major step in achieving this is to recount your own sexual auto-biography. This can be a fascinating endeavor. Tracing your own sexual history—your earliest memories of sexual awareness, the messages received from parents and friends, the patterns of sexual feeling and behavior you adopted in becoming an adult—can produce astonishing new insight. The beliefs you accepted, as well as those you rejected, become clearer. You can pinpoint patterns of action you adopted very early and that are now disruptive. And you can find aspects of your sexual self you like and wish to retain.

In the next few pages you will find some questions to guide you in sketching your autobiography. Respond to those that seem important to you. Let them prod your memory. You need not confine yourself to these questions; feel free to move in any direction that seems useful in order to identify the critical events and images that have shaped the sexual person you are today.

Although it is most useful to write out your autobiography, you may not have the privacy to do so. In that case, sit back and meditate. Pause after each question, close your eyes, and recall as much as you can about your sexual past. Look for any patterns that might emerge and for key experiences with some special influence. The more awareness you can develop about your sexual past, the more fruitful your exploration of sexual style is likely to be.

INFANCY: What are your earliest memories of sexual feelings and activities? Remember them in as much detail as you can recall. What sexual attitudes of your parents do you remember? Do you have images of seeing adult genitals? Of discovering the difference between boys and girls? Do you have any strong feelings, good or bad, about being a boy or a girl?

CHILDHOOD: Picture yourself as a child of elementary school age. What is it like in your family? What messages do you get from your parents about your sexuality? How are you supposed to act as a boy or a girl? How do you feel about the opposite sex? How do you feel about your body? What are your feelings about touching your genitals? Do you observe your own body? Have nudity in the family? Have sexual contact with siblings? Relatives? Other children? Animals? Have you been sexually molested? Seriously or subtly? What do you enjoy sexually and what do you fear or find difficult and confusing? Do you experience guilt about your sexual behavior or fantasies? Does religion influence your sexual attitudes? Does anything happen at school to affect you sexually?

ADOLESCENCE: Look back over your teen years. What are your feelings about yourself during puberty? About the way you look? About your changing sexual organs? About your role as male or female? How do you feel about the opposite sex? What worries you most? What kind of sex talk do you have with boys? With girls? With adults? How do your parents influence, or try to influence, your sexual behavior at this time? Are there any changes in their handling of sexual matters with you as you mature? Do you have more direct physical contact with them or less? Is there conversation with them about sex? What are your major feelings and experiences? Do you have important experiences with masturbation? Heavy petting? Intercourse? Animal contact? Sadism? Masochism? Same-sex contact? Oral-genital contact? Anal intercourse? Do you have any fantasies about any of these activities? Do you attach sexual fantasies to any objects, pictures, items of clothing? What experiences or fantasies give you feelings of guilt or abnormality? Which give you the most pain? Which give you the most enjoyment? Is there anything that you still today regret having done?

EARLY ADULTHOOD: Describe your sexual life in your late teens and early twenties. Are you trying out new sexual activities? If you did not lose your virginity in adolescence, describe how it happened now —or has it not yet happened? What most turns you on sexually now? Do your activities change radically when you leave your parents' home, or do they stay pretty much the same? How do you feel about the sexual style you have adopted? Do you relate to one sex or both sexes? To one partner or many partners? In private or in group situations? What do you like about your sexual relationships and what do you find to be unsatisfactory? Do you know what you want from sex and what in your past may be keeping you from getting what you want?

LATER ADULTHOOD: How have your frustrations and satisfactions changed from early adulthood? Have some sexual problems disappeared? Have new ones emerged? Have your earlier hopes and expectations been met? Would you like sex to be more important in your life or less? If you have a partner, do you have similar views about sex or not? If you have children, how much have your sexual ideas and actions changed while rearing them? Can you see any patterns in the family of your childhood reappearing in your present family situation? Are you happy with this, or are there some patterns you would like to change?

If you could change one thing in your sexual style, what would it be? What have you found that you really like about yourself sexually? In what actions and attitudes do you take pride? If your reply is "None," then look again. Are there really no aspects of your sexuality that you can affirm? A little self-affirmation at least is essential to this exploration of sexual values. (If you feel your sexual story provides you with nothing to approve, you may wish to consider consulting someone who can help you to work on the fundamental problem of self-acceptance. The method we have used in this book can help improve your self-image, but it makes no claim to provide therapy and healing.)

You have now looked briefly in the mirror at the style of your sexual self. You have stepped through the mirror to examine what lies behind your sexual image. Does a picture begin to form in your mind of who you are as a sexual person? Have you located any sources of tension in your current style? Just discovering the causes of some of the strains may help to ease them. But because discovery itself is often not enough, in future chapters we will suggest ways of sorting through various sexual tensions.

2

———————————————————

Juggling Sexual Values

Imagine a sexual style that allows unlimited freedom, commitment, variety, spontaneity, security, intimacy, privacy, flexibility, stability, fidelity, and excitement! Ridiculous, isn't it? No one way of living can possibly provide all those goodies, and certainly not all of them in equal measure. Different sexual styles reinforce different values. Any sexual style is something of a juggling act: you can keep several balls in the air at one time, but there is a limit. No matter how skillful you are, you can't keep too many things going at once. There must be some kind of balance in the items you put together.

If your sexual style is satisfying, it will provide for the values you most treasure. There will not be destructive conflict between what you *feel* to be right and what you *believe* to be right. Your style will reflect your genuine needs and desires, as well as any principles you deem important.

What Goes into Your Act

Volumes would be required to describe every variation of sexual style—and even then these styles would not be linked to your values. More helpful is a framework of choices that you can use to locate and evaluate your sexual style.

On the following pages there are descriptions of a number of people who have in various ways answered the five ticklish questions you asked yourself in the previous chapter. (As you read them, ignore the classifications in the right-hand margin. Cover them with a piece of paper until you have finished on page 18.) While you are reading the seven descriptions, consider the appeal of each style for you. Put a 1 and a 2 in the space by the two styles that appeal to you the most. Put a 6 and a 7 by the two that you like least. This does not necessarily mean that you would wish to change places with the person whose style is your first choice, but that of the people and styles presented here, this is the one you appreciate most. Don't be influenced by extraneous factors, such as the person's name or job. Concentrate on the style in each case. (If you have a partner, we suggest that you do this and the following exercise independently, consulting each other only after you have finished.)

_____ 1. James is a bachelor who works for a large volunteer organization. He travels extensively and enjoys seeing new places and making new friends. He long ago decided that he was not cut out for marriage. In fact, he cannot understand why people worry so much about sex. It's not all it's cracked up to be, and neither are most marriages—not if his glimpses of them are anything to go by. As far as he can see, a lot of pain could be avoided if people were less preoccupied with sex. He occasionally has sexual affairs, but he certainly never goes about seeking them. What's more, he always tells his partner that for him sex must be with "no strings attached." He has better things to do than to get his life messed up with sexual entanglements.

____ Expressive
_✓_ Nonexpressive
_✓_ Casual
____ Relational
____ Exclusive
_✓_ Nonexclusive
____ Procreative
_✓_ Nonprocreative

_____ 2. Beth is a young woman who is very serious about succeeding professionally. She believes that getting involved in an important relationship at this time could seriously hinder her efforts to get ahead. She might like a deep and permanent relationship in five or ten years, but right now she wants to remain "fancy free." However, she does enjoy an active sex life. She has a good time in bed and says, "It's been great. See you later!" She is careful and dis-

_✓_ Expressive
____ Nonexpressive
_✓_ Casual
____ Relational
____ Exclusive
_✓_ Nonexclusive
____ Procreative
_✓_ Nonprocreative

creet about her sexual activities, and so far this approach has worked well for her. She has had no difficulty finding willing partners to go along with her style of "sex only and nothing more."

_____ 3. Debby and Brad have been sexual partners for years. They enjoy each other's company immensely and spend most weekends together, but it is unlikely that they will ever get married. Both avoid the heavy commitment that marriage represents. They value their freedom too much to be tied down by children or the demands that marriage seems to make. They like being able to pursue other relationships, including other sexual relationships. They enjoy a high degree of sexual activity and include a lot of playacting in their lovemaking. Although there is some novelty in sex with others, they get the most satisfaction from the routines they have developed together.

√ Expressive
___ Nonexpressive
___ Casual
√ Relational
___ Exclusive
√ Nonexclusive
___ Procreative
√ Nonprocreative

_____ 4. In the several years Sue and Ray have lived together, they have occasionally discussed marriage, but since they are not intending to have children, they see no point to it. They do, however, have a highly prized and committed relationship. They see sexual fidelity as the main proof of their commitment. Reserving intercourse just for each other makes their relationship special, even though sex is not their main activity together. They believe that too much sex leads to an obsession. If you just take it easy, have a lot of other interests, and keep sex as an occasional bedtime activity, then things work out pretty well.

___ Expressive
√ Nonexpressive
___ Casual
√ Relational
√ Exclusive
___ Nonexclusive
___ Procreative
√ Nonprocreative

_____ 5. Marge and Tom have been married for ten years and have three children. They very much enjoy their family and devote at least one day each weekend entirely to activities

√ Expressive
___ Nonexpressive
___ Casual

with the children. They feel that their love would not have been complete without them. They value their sexual relationship highly, but they also feel it is good to have an outside sexual "fling" occasionally. These escapades supply novelty and excitement and prevent boredom. Moreover, Marge and Tom sometimes return to each other with some new technique to spice up their own lovemaking. Since they take precautions not to have children with their casual lovers, they do not see how any harm is done. They keep firmly in mind that their priorities are with each other and their children.

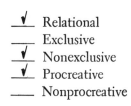

_✓_ Relational
____ Exclusive
_✓_ Nonexclusive
_✓_ Procreative
____ Nonprocreative

____ 6. Gerald and Claire wanted a family and now have four school-age children. Their whole life seems to revolve around the family. Once they had the number of children they wanted, their sexual activity dwindled considerably. Sex no longer seemed to serve a definite purpose, and there were lots of other things to take its place. Once or twice they picked up a magazine article on sexual enrichment and tried out some of the suggestions, but basically neither of them enjoyed it very much. It has never occurred to either of them to get involved sexually with anyone else. They really get the greatest satisfaction from sharing their love and devotion in what they do together with the children.

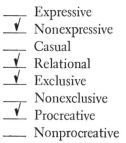

____ Expressive
_✓_ Nonexpressive
____ Casual
_✓_ Relational
_✓_ Exclusive
____ Nonexclusive
_✓_ Procreative
____ Nonprocreative

____ 7. John and Carolyn are always together. Although they have been married for years, they still appear like newlyweds to their friends. The two of them believe there are good reasons why the magic has remained. First, they decided not to have children, and second, they have a terrific sex life. They take long, soapy baths together, give each other shower massages, and use various vibrators and other sexual aids, experimenting in all sorts of

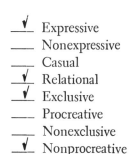

_✓_ Expressive
____ Nonexpressive
____ Casual
_✓_ Relational
_✓_ Exclusive
____ Procreative
____ Nonexclusive
_✓_ Nonprocreative

ways in their lovemaking. Since there is so much novelty and excitement between them, they do not feel the need of any outside sexual relationships and devote all their energy and creativity to each other.

When you are satisfied with your ratings of life-styles, look at the classifications in the margins next to the descriptions. Each style is marked with checks, making obvious the choices that have been made about four of the ticklish questions. This will provide you with labels for the styles you like, don't like, or are unclear about. The labels are of course less important than an understanding of the variables they represent. If you apply these labels to yourself, do so only in a very tentative way. This is not a scientific test, and you don't want to box yourself in. These are simply shorthand labels to simplify your consideration of a wide variety of complex issues.

When you have completed your ratings, put them aside for the moment and look at the following list of values. These are items regularly mentioned by counselors and other experts as desirable for sexual or relational satisfaction. Which do you feel are most important for your own fulfillment?

Put a 3 in the space next to any value that is very important to you. This is a value you take pride in and are willing to make an important life goal. Put a 2 next to any value that is somewhat or slightly important to you. If you feel an item is not important or is even harmful, put a 1 in the space.

How important is . . . ?

_____ Freedom/spontaneity

_____ Trust

_____ Openness/honesty

_____ Intimacy/closeness

_____ Equality

_____ Joy/pleasure

_____ Personal growth

_____ Commitment

_____ Realistic expectations

_____ Sexual fidelity/exclusiveness

■
      _____ Independence/privacy
      _____ Sexual satisfaction
      _____ Security/stability
      _____ Sexual excitement/novelty

Some of these are hard to estimate. You may have been tempted to place a 3 next to most of them. Remember that you are a juggler. Realism suggests that you can't have everything. Try going back and choosing only four that are most important to you.

When you have completed this list, turn back to the seven descriptions at the beginning of the chapter. Take the life-style you ranked first—the one that appealed to you most. Read the description again, and try to imagine how well this life-style supports the values you rated most highly. Do the same for the life-style you ranked second most appealing. Do the life-styles you liked seem to support the values you consider most important?

If so, you have (whether or not you are aware of it) a pretty good notion of what you want your sexual style to be. As you read the rest of the book, you will be able to explore your style more fully. You may not be living the sexual style you want, you may have many questions and uncertainties, and you may not know how to express your sexual style to others. All these topics will be addressed later in the book. If there is a marked difference between the way you rated the life-styles and the way you rated the values, you will want to look around for an explanation. For example, if you especially liked John and Carolyn yet rated independence and privacy highly, something is awry.

There are several possibilities to consider. One of the most common is that your head and your heart are not in quite the same mood. The descriptions are heavier on emotional content, and the value items are perhaps more abstract, more rational. What you like or feel comes out more in the descriptions; what you believe or think comes out more in the value items. If that is the case, you have a decision to make. Which do you trust more—your emotions or your intellect?

Another possibility is that the sexual style you like on paper is different from the one you are pursuing in reality. That may create some discrepancies in your ratings on the two scales. Tension between what we want or believe and how we act can be upsetting. If you feel this tension, can you identify the values you stressed in your ratings that are not emphasized in your current sexual style, or vice versa? Take a look at the list of values again.

This time, mark how much of each you feel you *now have* in your sexual relationship. A rating of 3 means you have a great deal; 2 means you have some; 1 means you have little or none. (Rate what you have regardless of how much you want; you may feel you have too much security or too much variety.)

How much do you have . . . ?

_____ Freedom/spontaneity

_____ Trust

_____ Openness/honesty

_____ Intimacy/closeness

_____ Equality

_____ Joy/pleasure

_____ Personal growth

_____ Commitment

_____ Realistic expectations

_____ Sexual fidelity/exclusiveness

_____ Independence/privacy

_____ Sexual satisfaction

_____ Security/stability

_____ Sexual excitement/novelty

Compare your ratings on this list with your previous ones. Are there values that you rated "very important" in the life-style descriptions that you feel are not strongly present in your current sexual style? These are ones that you will want to ponder with care as you work through the book. Do you want to continue to act on the basis of the values you have currently, or do you wish to change your style to include values you find more appealing? All of us are constantly curried or cajoled by conflicting models of behavior and belief. If you locate these areas of conflict, you can begin to resolve the issues that might lead to the pursuit of a more satisfying sexual style.

A third source of confusion may be the presence of negative values. The list of values you have been considering are all positive; each one is good (except perhaps some that you can have in excess). However, for each item there is a corresponding negative value. If trust is good, lack of trust is bad. But notice that there is a subtle difference. Suppose you think trust is only slightly important. Does it follow that you think distrust is only slightly negative? No. You may not believe that a lot of trust is necessary yet feel that any distrust will end a sexual relationship.

Look at the list below. Each item is the opposite—the negative—of a value in the first list. How negative are they for you? Use 3 to indicate extremely negative, 2 to indicate somewhat negative, and 1 to indicate only slightly negative or unimportant.

How bad is . . . ?

____ Jealousy

____ Possessiveness

____ Secrecy

____ Distrust

____ Sexual infidelity

____ Sexual inadequacy

____ Inequality

____ Dependence

____ Boredom

____ Rigidity

You might add your own list of what you especially don't like, things that influence your sexual style decisively. What about physical abuse, exploitation, manipulation, or just lack of taste or imagination in sexual play?

Compare this list with your ratings of life-styles on pages 15–18. Take the life-styles you liked most. Would living in these ways help you avoid the important negatives? In choosing a sexual style, could the negative risks tip the balance between one style and another for you? For example, you may regard jealousy as very harmful but at the same time find that a style you feel is susceptible to jealousy nevertheless fulfills many of the positive values you wish to pursue. If so, do you want to pursue this style in hopes that its positive values will overcome this very harmful risk, or would you prefer to pursue another style that you believe still has a number of positive values but is not so apt to encourage jealousy? Are you aware of having made compromises such as this, of having balanced positive gains against negative risks? Go over the list of negative values, and ask yourself how much they are part of your current sexual style.

If you have a partner who has also rated the styles and values, now is the time to compare your responses. This may be a bit scary, but there is no way to improve, or even maintain, a relationship without both persons participating in the change. For you to change your sexual style alone or to maintain it insensitively against your partner's feelings may leave your partner at least perplexed and, more likely, feeling angry and distraught. Nevertheless, it is pointless to hide real differences in feeling and conviction. There is less reason to fear discussing these tensions than pretending they do not exist. Rather, a new awareness of differences that may be causing tension in your sexual relationship provides a splendid opportunity to move toward a new way of being together. Of course, there is always the possibility that such differences are insurmountable. If that seems to you now to be the case, stay with the next few chapters, where these styles are dealt with in more detail. You may find the differences are less when the fine features of each are in focus. In any case, there will be an opportunity in Chapter 13 to struggle directly with the problems of conflicting sexual styles within a partnership.

Your Special Blend

Freedom, commitment, intimacy, pleasure—rather slippery words, are they not? You may have had trouble getting a grip on some of them. They are easier to grasp when linked to some action that provides a clue to their precise meaning. For example, a dictionary definition of *fidelity* is not very helpful to a couple who have quite different ideas about it. When one person says, "I'm always true to you, darling, in my fashion," the other may respond, "So long, it's been good to know you."

> For the first couple of years of their marriage, Don and Harriet lived rather conventionally. Harriet remained at home, and Don returned punctually from work every evening for supper. They would then read or watch television. Gradually boredom set in. Don began to feel restricted by this routine. He started staying downtown after work to have a drink with a friend. At length it was apparent to Harriet that he was spending time with one or two of the secretaries from the office. When Don began without warning not to show up for dinner, she determined to have it out with him. She intended to question him calmly, but she immediately broke down in tears, reproaching him for giving up his commitment to her and throwing over their marriage.

Don replied in dismay that of course he was still committed to her and that he had no intention of getting a divorce. He just wanted more freedom, he said. Harriet, now furious, retorted that unless Don stopped being so free and returned to his earlier habits, she would seek a divorce.

With whom are you more sympathetic in this tug-of-war?

Don 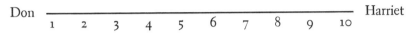 Harriet

Place yourself somewhere on this line. If you support Don wholeheartedly, put a mark at Don's end of the line. If you fully agree with Harriet, put a mark at her end. If your attitude falls somewhere between the two, place yourself accordingly, moving the mark closer to the person with whom you more nearly agree. (Would it make a difference if Don were Donna taking more freedom and Harriet were Harry resisting?)

This little scenario presents a common problem, even though these two seem to be handling it with uncommon ineptitude. There can be extreme tension between two values, each of which is desirable when considered by itself. Don wants more freedom and spontaneity. Great! But Harriet wants more dependability and commitment. Oh! And such tensions are not limited to conflict between two people. The dilemma may be even more devilish when the tug-of-war is within you. You may, for example, want a lot of sexual excitement and variety. Great! But you may also want the security of one constant and intimate relationship. That may be difficult to manage.

As long as we stick to vague generalities like *freedom* and *fidelity*, we may fail even to recognize the presence of these tensions. Actions like Don's bring the difficulty into focus. Of course, it is not necessary to achieve clarity so painfully. You can determine the precise meaning of the values you appreciate by finding the actions that for you measure their meaning and importance.

How do you measure the values you prize? How do you measure commitment, for example? By the number of hours you spend with a partner, by taking care of him or her physically or financially, by being sexually exclusive? Think of some concrete behaviors that measure commitment for you.

Now consider freedom. What is freedom for you? Being able to go where you want when you want? Having sex with whomever you want? Being able to buy anything you want? Think of some concrete behaviors that represent freedom for you. Are there any tensions between the behavior that represents commitment for you and the behavior that represents freedom?

Clearly, freedom and commitment are bigger concepts than these questions indicate. Nevertheless, all abstract values are ultimately translated into our lives by the very real limits we all face. There are only so many hours in the day, only so much money in our pockets, only so many things we can be doing at any one time. You are always making choices between one thing, one action, or one person and another. Sometimes these choices are easy. Other times they are not. You feel a tug-of-war going on inside you. At these times you are apt to be experiencing a value conflict.

Look at the following pairs of values that are often in tension. Think of some concrete behaviors that *for you* support each value. Then check the pairs that create tension in your life. Are there any pairs here—or others that you can think of—where one value always wins the tug-of-war?

Commitment . . . . Freedom

Privacy . . . . Intimacy

Sexual novelty . . . . Permanence

Openness . . . . Privacy

Personal growth . . . . Security

Independence . . . . Sexual fidelity/exclusiveness

Other . . . . Other

By now you should know a good bit about what you want in your sexual style. You know not only which values matter most to you but also whether you want more of any value. You also may have discovered some values that are in tension in your life. If so, don't despair—isolating your conflicts is the first step toward resolving them. In the next chapters we shall take a tour of sexual styles. We shall explore the meaning of expressive and nonexpressive sexual style; we'll talk about casual sex (where love is unimportant) and relational sex (where love matters a great deal); we'll explore what children mean, or do not mean, to your sexual style. As we do so, we'll help you answer the questions we've raised.

3

Getting In Deep

Are you a deep-water swimmer, or do you prefer to stroll along in the tide pools? Some people are sexual swimmers who are out to enjoy the depths. They take in the dramatic beauty of these depths and then return to shore pleasantly tired, already looking forward to another day. Others are waders who like the occasional stroll along the rocky shore, now and then dipping a foot in a quiet pool, watching tiny creatures scurrying in the water at their feet. The sexual style of the swimmer is expressive; that of the wader is nonexpressive.

You probably have an idea whether you are a swimmer or a wader sexually. If you are clear about that, this chapter will be an exploration of what it means to make sex an important life priority. If you are not yet clear, then in these pages you can gauge how much intensity you want in your sexual style.

Sex Front and Center

Sex is important. No one who disagrees with this statement is apt to read this book. But what do we mean if we say that sex has great importance in human life?

We might mean that sex is the best way to sell deodorant or a new car. After all, sex is a prime ingredient in most advertising. Notice, however, that using it commercially actually makes sex secondary, a means to something else. The seller gets a profit, the consumer gets a fantasy, but nobody gets into bed with anybody else. Only indirectly, as an image maker and marketing gimmick, does sexy advertising illuminate the importance of sex: the fact that we are so easily manipulated by sexually suggestive images may rest upon some unfathomed feeling that our happiness is somehow at stake in the way we handle our sexuality.

The size of the pornography market might also point to the centrality of sex. Whether it is a $4-billion-a-year business in the United States or only $150 million, as various estimates run, that is a lot of money going for materials intended to titillate the erotic spots on the human imagination. But even more money, about $20 billion, is spent on alcoholic beverages. Does this mean that alcohol is more important in human life than sex? Certainly not. It may be very important to many people, but it is hardly central to human existence.

Sex is more basic than is suggested by its commercialization. Sex is a natural physiological function. The human male ordinarily has an erection about every sixty to eighty minutes while asleep. Females lubricate vaginally during sleep. Babies are born male or female, and they don't seem to need anyone to tell them what to do about it. At birth they already have many of the physical responses of their sex. Girl babies lubricate vaginally soon after birth, and boys have erections almost as soon as they are born. Probably both male erections and female vaginal lubrications take place even prior to birth.[1] These tiny creatures will be involved the rest of their lives in exploring the nature and meaning of being girl or boy, woman or man. Awake or asleep, working or playing, tired or refreshed, in childhood or old age, *to be human is to be sexual.*

This does not mean that to be human is to be as sexual as possible. Breathing, sleeping, and eating are all natural functions, but it would be foolish to interpret this to mean that we should breathe as much as possible or eat as much as possible. More may or may not be better. Sexuality is one natural function over which we have a high degree of conscious control. The survival of the human race has so far depended upon sex, but personal survival is a different matter. Unlike breathing, you do not die if you have no orgasm, even if it might occasionally feel that way. (But whereas genital, orgasmic sex is not a physiological necessity, the warmth of human contact is indispensable. Babies in institutions that provide little human care have a much higher death rate than those in institutions where babies are at least washed, cleaned, and fed by hand.)[2]

"To be human is to be sexual" does not mean being sexual in a particular way. Sexual urges can be ignored or squashed and pounded into all kinds of odd shapes and sizes. Our natures as persons may be shaped or sometimes distorted by these various sexual shapes, but personal humanity is neither created nor destroyed by this variety of sexual manners. We can mold our sexuality to fulfill our personal and social needs. The somewhat barbaric comparison often made between eating and sex has an important point behind it. We have to eat, but we can choose the manner in which we shall eat. You can grab a quick bite at a snack bar with no other purpose than to satisfy your body's need. Or you can with friends or family have a leisurely meal by candlelight with wine and music. You then satisfy needs of affection or companionship as well as the need for nourishment. In fact, the emotional needs you are fulfilling may at times be more important to you than the physical needs being met.

In a similar way, a given sexual act can be simply the means to resolve a physical drive, or it can be the means to satisfy an emotional need—say, intimacy or affection or pleasure. In the wide range of styles by which people act out their sexual being, the very meaning of existence is signified. To be sexual in a certain way is to be human in a certain way. Consider the meaning of these sexual acts: "consummation" of a marriage, "hoping to have a baby"; "balling" by a teenager trying to "find out what it's like"; "making love" by an elderly couple married for forty years. Even the words we use to describe sexual intercourse say something about the way we are living in the world.

What words do you use to describe intercourse?
Do you use different words in different situations?
What do these words say about the meaning of sex in your life?

"To be human is to be sexual." If we are not the helpless agents of a drive the satisfaction of which is directly dictated by biology, then there are, happily, a wide variety of ways by which we can live satisfactory sexual lives. To be very active and to have sex near the center of existence is not a necessity but a choice. To have a take-it-or-leave-it style of sexual life is equally a matter of choice.

How important is sex in your life? To answer that question, let's first look at what you think about sexual pleasure.

What Is Pleasure to Me?

Pleasure has a role in your life. It may be the pot of gold you are always seeking. It may be the tempter threatening to lure you away from the more important goals of life. Your sexual choices are influenced by how you view pleasure. Therefore, consider the choices you make about pleasure from day to day.

First, do you seek sexual pleasure? If in the last chapter you rated highly pleasure, joy, sexual satisfaction, sexual excitement, then pleasure is very likely one of your measures of the desirability of a given act. Jane's favorite activity is tennis. She will pass up an invitation to bed for a quick set on the tennis court. She makes this decision on the basis of taste: tennis gives her more pleasure. You can make all your decisions by estimating the pleasure involved for yourself and/or others. Or pleasure can be just one of your considerations. I choose to make love at any time of day it pleases me, but not with anyone who happens to please me. Other values are important to my choice of partner. To still other people pleasure is not a goal at all but the happy by-product of achieving other goals. "I don't seek relationships in order to get sexual pleasure. I want a deep relationship, and pleasure—sexual and emotional—results naturally."

Second, how much sexual pleasure do you seek? You may say, "The more the better. If sex is good, then the more sex the better." On the other hand, you may say, "I can have too much of a good thing. If I overeat, then I suffer unpleasant consequences. I enjoy a good meal, or good sex, more if I don't overindulge."

Third, whose sexual pleasure do you seek? You may seek your own pleasure primarily and only consider whether or not you are actively doing harm to other people: "Here I am with a willing sexual partner, hurting no one, so why shouldn't I enjoy myself?" Or you may make increasing another's pleasure a primary goal: "What would *you* like to do?" If you believe in the twin dangers of exploitation and philanthropy, you will probably try to avoid both sexual egotism and the mother-hen syndrome by seeking a blend of self and other's pleasure.

Finally, when do you want to have your sexual pleasure—now or later? You may feel that concentrating on pleasure now is likely to bring later un-happiness or block the attainment of more important long-term goals. If you spend too much time lolling in bed, you won't get that promotion which would bring greater happiness in the long run. Or that affair might be fun, but the risk that it would disrupt your happy family life is too great. On the other hand, you may believe that for too long we have been told to put off till tomorrow the pleasure we could have today. Frequently tomorrow never comes. Thus, pleasure should be grasped when it's avail-able: "Gather ye rosebuds while ye may."

Circle your immediate response to each of these questions:

1. Do I seek pleasure?

   Yes! Yes! Yes!   Well, sometimes.   No, never!

2. What kinds of pleasures do I seek?

   Intellectual   Physical   Sexual   Emotional

   Simple   Material   Elaborate

   —————— ?   —————— ?   —————— ?

3. In what amount?

   The more the better.   Easy does it.

4. For whom?

   Myself alone.   Myself and others.   Others only.

5. When?

   Right now!   Soon.   Later, later.

If you want to qualify some of your responses, go ahead. Your answers to these questions determine how you choose to act or not to act from day to day. They tell you something about why your sex life is organized the way it is. The way you value pleasure is one of the important elements in the complex of values that make up your sexual style.

Waders and Swimmers

There are twenty-four hours in your day, no more and no less. How much of that time you invest in sex is a good measure of the importance of sex in your life. Similarly, you have only so much energy. No fantasies about bionic sexuality will change that. If you feel that sex is very important to you, the test of that attitude is how you spend your time and energy.

Below you will find two pies. The first of them will show how you spend your time and energy now. The second can represent how you would ideally like to spend your time and energy. Divide the first pie into slices according to how much time you spend in each of the major kinds of daily activities. Exclude normal working hours (about eight hours a day, five days a week) and sleeping time. Include overtime worked, however. The pie is supposed to reveal how you spend time that is at your discretion—free time.

Label the slices of the pie, representing the amount of time you spend in each of these ways:

> H for *house* (taking care of your house, room, or apartment: cleaning, paying bills, making repairs)
>
> V for *vocation* (bettering yourself vocationally beyond required work or study)
>
> A for *alone* (taking care of yourself or enjoying yourself: washing your hair, tending clothes, reading a book)
>
> F for *family* (taking care of, or doing things with, a family)
>
> O for *others* (social activities with other people)
>
> C for *companionship* (nonsexual activities with a sexual partner: talking, going to the theater, swimming)
>
> S for *sex* (activities that are directly sensual or sexual with a sexual partner)

Reality Pie

Now, using the same labels, divide the second pie according to how you would ideally like to be spending your time.

Ideal Pie

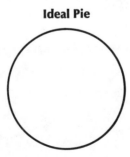

Is your ideal pie very different from your reality pie? Could your ideal pie be made a reality, or would trying be foolish idealism? Do you have to spend that extra time at work, or do you do it because you really want to? Are you a compulsive housekeeper? Do you wish you weren't? In what sections of the pie are your major enjoyments located? How large a part does sex play in your life? Do you want it to be more or less?

You may have found that sex took up a very small portion of your reality pie and that there were other activities that you wanted to expand in your ideal pie. In this case, you have chosen a nonexpressive sexual style and are content with it. Great! You can choose from a wide variety of satisfying goals, organizing your life around them to such an extent that sex has little importance for you. If this book concentrates on sex as an important life goal, this is not to put a negative value judgment on nonexpressive sexual styles: it is, rather, because we cannot here deal with all nonsexual life-style options.

On the other hand, you may have been content with the size of the slice representing sexual or sensual activities but still wish that the time spent could be more rewarding. Good point! The quality of your sex life is measured not only by the time you put into it. The way you are present to your partner while you are doing other things may be a mark of sexual expressiveness. Conversely, overt sexual acts may be empty of sexual feeling or meaning. It is very common to long for a deeper sensual existence. This is the purpose of the further exercises in this chapter—to explore some modes of sexual sensitivity that you may wish to consider.

Getting In Deeper

For someone with a casual view of sex, an expressive style might mean having sex with a wide variety of partners. Listen to one man explain why he has chosen this way:

"I seem to want more sexual variety than one person—no matter how good—could ever really give me. Sometimes I yearn for a svelte, trim body with firm muscles that offer some resistance to my caress. Other times I want to be able to sink slowly into mounds of soft, yielding flesh. I also enjoy being a different sort of lover with different women. With some I am aggressive and domineering, with others I am soft and languorous. I get a real 'high' out of being able to switch around."

Close your eyes for a moment and imagine yourself pursuing such a style. Dream about having a number of sexual partners, each of whom brings out a different side of your sexual nature.

Is this difficult or uncomfortable to think about? Or is this easy to fantasize but difficult to imagine carrying out in reality? Would you like to be such a person? Would you enjoy such a person as a lover? As a friend?

Another way of sprucing up sexual expressiveness would be to have a "sex only" affair. Listen to this woman who took a lover to get the sex life she desired:

"My husband and I love each other, but he is very busy and really isn't very interested in sex. For a long time this caused a lot of pain between us. Then one day he volunteered that I could do what I wanted with my own time. . . .

"Now I have a really neat lover. It's strictly sex. We meet once or twice a week for some pretty wild and way-out sex. My husband doesn't like to fool around, but with my lover I can have all the excitement I want—touching everything, sucking this . . . licking that. . . . In fact, recently we decided we would get a kick out of working our way through all the positions in the *Kama Sutra*. We are really having fun.

"Good sex is important to me. I think I've found a way to have it without breaking up my marriage."

How about this style? Imagine having two sexual partners, one of whom mainly fulfills emotional needs and the other of whom satisfies your sexual desires. Think about your lover. Imagine all that you might do with this person sexually. How easy is this to fantasize? Does the thought feel like idle fancy, or does it feel more like an unfulfilled side of yourself? Are you revolted by the idea of sex with no other relationship to that person? Is there any way you could change the fantasy to make this style more attractive to you?

Obviously, having more than one sexual partner is not going to jazz up your sexual style if you feel as dull with one partner as the last. Or you may be upset and repulsed by the idea of having more than one person in your sex life. Whether one partner or many, sexual expressiveness has to do with a special erotic quality that is yours and yours alone. If you want to be more expressive sexually, there are things you can do about it. Have you ever sat down with your partner and looked at a manual of sexual technique—not necessarily to try everything the book suggests and certainly not to attempt to perform up to an implied level of sexual excellence, but just to see what turns you on and what you can do to turn your partner on? A book like Alex Comfort's *The Joy of Sex* can be great fun. Or you might look at an erotic art book.

If you really want to be sexually more expressive, then you are probably willing to try something quite new. What about a soft, caressing massage with oils or lotions? You can give a massage that caresses the erotic places as much as aching muscles, using a touch that expresses sensual delight, giving your partner as much pleasure as your imagination can devise, moving your hands gently and smoothly, dangling your hair deftly here and there, touching now and again with tongue or cheek. Or again, lie back and let your partner pleasure you sensually—slowly, gently, with little variations that catch the mood of your being together. Could you—would you—take the time and ensure the privacy for this?

Then what about intercourse itself? Is it just "Wham, bam, thank you, ma'am"? Is the "sex act" just that, an act performed self-consciously and a little bit tediously? Or is it "getting it on" with another person, letting the rhythm of your bodies mark time for an orgasmic crescendo? Is it "just another lay," or is it "once more with feeling"? Is it an invariable routine, or something that encourages you to dream about the other side of the rainbow? You do not have to be an amorous genius to put a little flair into sex. You may need to let go a little, forget yourself some, cease being an observer of yourself. You will need to take the time for it, and you will need to play around with different sexual moods, expressing the needs and desires that you are feeling at a given time or that you sense in your partner. Imagine being aggressive and dominant with your partner this time, leading him or her through a series of caresses and positions that satisfy the way you feel. And then imagine another time being very relaxed and passive, accepting whatever your partner offers, letting yourself be led. Imagine mutually masturbating to orgasm today, perhaps using your mouths, but tomorrow making love in a completely novel position.

Do these thoughts and suggestions excite you, or are they somehow disturbing? Do they seem perfectly natural? Are they part of your lovemaking style already? Have any of these suggestions triggered any ideas about how you might increase the expressiveness of your own sexual style? Or did you find yourself resisting most of them?

At this point you might have a dialogue with yourself about how expressive you want your sexual style to be. This may seem silly or uncomfortable at first, but you may be amazed at the insight this exercise can provide.

> Put a pillow on a chair in front of you and tell it all you would like about having a more expressive style. Then move onto the pillow and respond to your expressive self. Be your nonexpressive self, and tell your expressive self all the reasons for *not* being more expressive. Now move back to your original position and respond to the arguments of your nonexpressive self. Then go back to the pillow and reply to your expressive self's arguments. Do this several times. Does one side get stronger and win the argument? Do some of the statements you make sound convincing and others rather hollow?

Getting It Together with Someone Else

It is one thing to be clear about your own sexual expressiveness; it is quite another thing to get it together with the style of another person. Yet all but solo sex requires just that. The next several exercises are structured so that you can explore the details of your sexual enjoyment in relation to the style of a partner. Whether with a partner or not, first find your own feelings on each strategy before comparing them with those of a partner. However, if you do not have a significant sexual partner, it will be useful to study the strategies with another person. Bouncing your feelings and ideas off those of someone else is often the most effective way to find out what you really feel or believe.

> Below is a chart that lists parts of the body generally considered to give erotic pleasure or to receive it. Across the top are male parts; down the side are female parts.* There are a couple of extra boxes in which you can put any body parts where you personally feel you get erotic pleasure (toes, feet, back of the neck, thighs, and so on). Cross out all boxes that you feel represent improbable or impossible contact. (Can you really rub anuses?) Then put a plus sign (+) in every box

---

* Space limitations have prevented us from dealing with homosexuality in the depth it deserves. However, we suggest that homosexual readers alter the heterosexual language of this and subsequent exercises to fit their situation. It is our belief that the major questions and value issues raised in this book apply to homosexuals as well as heterosexuals. We only regret that homosexual readers will have to struggle beyond the straight language to the issues raised.

representing contact you enjoy. For example, if you enjoy a male hand on a female breast, put a plus sign in the box where these two possibilities intersect. If you not only enjoy this contact but want more of it, put two pluses in the box. Put a minus sign $(-)$ in every box that represents contact you do not enjoy very much. Put two minuses if you feel you would like less of this contact than you are currently having. If you do this chart with a partner, do not let the other person see your chart until you have both completed it.

Erotic Contact

Female Body Parts	Male Body Parts								
	Mouth	Hand	Ear	Nipple	Penis	Scrotum	Anus		
Mouth									
Hand									
Ear									
Breast									
Clitoris									
Vagina									
Anus									

Now here is a list of sexual activities that are sometimes considered unusual or even bizarre. Go down the list and put a 1 by those that turn you on a great deal, a 2 by those that give you a mild turn-on, a 3 by those you feel neutral about, a 4 by those you have a slight distaste for, and a 5 by those that really repulse you. If you have a regular sexual partner, go through the list again, marking the activities this time *as you think your partner would.* If at all possible, have your partner do this exercise too. Before looking at your ratings, your partner should go down the list, marking each item once according to his or her own preference and once according to how he or she thinks you marked it for yourself.

　　a. Masturbation of myself while my partner is watching
　　b. Oral-genital sex to orgasm
　　c. Intercourse with the woman on top

   d. Intercourse in the "doggy" position
   e. Looking at explicit sexual materials together
   f. Anal intercourse
   g. Painting one another's bodies
   h. Erotic massage
   i. Seductive dress or stripping routines
   j. Any other item of your own

When you are both finished, compare your lists. How accurate were your perceptions of each other? Were there any surprises? Are there any things that you think you might like to do that you have not tried? Are there any things that you have been doing that you would like to stop?

The preceding chart and list can provide a wealth of information to be mined for the enrichment of any sexual relationship. If two of you do the exercises and compare notes, it is possible to find out what activities you would both like more of, what ones you would both like less of, and what ones you have differing feelings about. Whether you continue those you differ on probably depends to some extent on how distasteful or repugnant one partner finds the activity. You may be occasionally willing to tolerate something that is mildly distasteful if it gives your partner a great deal of pleasure, but not if the distaste is strong. The deep revulsion of one partner will sully the pleasure of the other.

You may find it very uncomfortable or embarrassing to talk about these things. The words may come with great difficulty: we rarely give ourselves permission to talk about explicitly sexual matters. If you are tongue-tied about sex, you can loosen your tongue a little by playing around with sex words.

1. Write the word or words that are particularly difficult or uncomfortable to say at the top of a piece of paper. With your partner try to think of five to ten other words or phrases that mean the same thing. These can be slang words, scientific words, or euphemisms, nice words that mean essentially the same thing. Now go through this list and choose the words or phrases that you both like best.

2. Choose a specific sexual word—either a scientific one or a slang one— and try making up some tongue twisters using that word. For example, "Peter's penis packs a punch." "Carol's clitoris collects callouses from constant caressing." "Tim tickled Tillie's tits till Tillie's twat twisted." Repeat them to each other.

These exercises may seem childish, but getting comfortable with a sexual language is serious business. We need to develop a climate in which to talk about explicit sexual matters with greater ease.

Finally, evaluate where all these discussions leave you. Do you want to leave your sexual style as it is? Do you want to devote the same amount of time to it but change the character or quality of the sexual relationship? Or have you decided you would like to devote more time or creativity to exploring new behaviors?

If you decide that you wish to increase the amount of time you devote to sexually related activities, then obviously something on that time pie you made earlier in this chapter has to change. What will it be? Many women complain that the new emphasis on expressive sexuality has just placed one more demand on their lives. They must now not only do everything they were expected to do in the past, but must hold down a career and still appear fresh and ready for extensive foreplay and an orgasm at bedtime. Some men, in turn, feel excessive performance demands on them. They feel they are being made responsible for a woman's reaching orgasm. It is no doubt a mistake to pile up demands either on yourself or on your partner.

> How much extra time a day or a week would you need to enrich your sex life? What must be done so that you and your partner both can approach your new program in a relaxed state? What would you be willing to give up in your current schedule so as to make more time for sex play? If it is your partner's schedule that is too full, what task would you be willing to assume so that your partner has more time and energy available? In short, how much are you willing to invest in making your sex life better?

If you are not in a primary relationship, increasing sexual expressiveness may require an even greater reworking of priorities. A single person may have to invest a lot of time and energy in cultivating new, or developing old, relationships that permit sexual expressiveness. This may leave less time and energy available for other activities that are enjoyable. In this case, it is necessary to decide how you would reorder your reality pie to make this time and energy available. What specifically are you willing to downgrade in order to upgrade sex in your life?

Dissatisfaction arises when you want either more or less than you currently have. Contentment comes from working out a style that is satisfying to you or to you and your partner in getting your sexual style aligned with your deepest desires.

4

■━━━■

Solo Sex

What if you are "horny" and there is no one else around? What do you do if you are left unsatisfied after the tension of a sexual encounter? Take a cold shower? Rush on quickly to some other exciting endeavor? Or take time to give yourself some pleasure and satisfaction? Is solo sex a part of your sexual style? How do you feel about being your own sexual partner?

Feeling Around for Feelings about Masturbation

Pimples, black heels, madness, impotence—an exhaustive list of warnings to masturbators would fill volumes. Actually, these terrible consequences of masturbation are either imaginary or the product of socialized shame. Many of the alarms would be comical if so many people—even medical students—did not still believe them.[1] The warnings have not stopped people from masturbating, but they have been extremely effective in producing feelings of guilt and shame about sexuality in general and masturbation in particular.

Deeply embedded feelings of shame usually cannot be dissolved by the mere acquisition of knowledge. Thus, children and even lovers frequently get one message from our behavior while we intend to give another. You may be quite aware that sex researcher Dr. Alfred Kinsey found masturbation to be very common and ventured the opinion that it had generally positive effects. You may even know that there has been substantial research supporting the role of masturbation in sexual functioning—that some research suggests masturbation reduces tension in young men and other research reports masturbation to be the sexual activity in which women generally reach orgasm most easily. In sum, you may be quite clear that masturbation has been proclaimed "normal." Nevertheless, you may still retain negative attitudes that stem from far back in your past.

Just as information alone does not form our attitudes, neither does it determine our values. One study shows no significant difference in emotional stability between females who masturbate frequently and those who do not. Another finds males who masturbate frequently to be very slightly higher on a neuroticism scale and to have intercourse less often than infrequent masturbators.[2] Do we conclude from this that women ought to masturbate and men ought not? Of course not. Even if all the research available pronounced masturbation harmless or beneficial (and most does come to such conclusions), that still would not mean that you personally *should* masturbate. Such a judgment would be another instance of the reverse moralism that replaces old sexual "oughts" with new ones. Making masturbation mandatory is as foolish as forbidding it. For example, you might want to refrain from masturbation for religious reasons, or you may find other modes of sexual expression so satisfying as to make masturbation unappealing.

Me and My Body

Suppose you have considered the information on masturbation and have decided that masturbation is all right, and yet your experience from childhood or youth still makes you feel anxious and guilty about sexual solos. You would like to feel more at ease. One of the first things to do is to explore the quality and flexibility of your feelings about your body.

What is your relationship to your body? Are you happily inseparable or barely on speaking terms? If it is practical for you, do this exercise now, but if not, do it the next time you are undressing.

Stand nude in front of the mirror. Take a long, careful look at your body. Follow its contours; study its texture and color. Appreciate its special character and quality. While you are doing this, say over and over to yourself, "I am my body, I am my body . . ." Get into the feeling you and it are the same thing. You think with your body, you feel with it, you hope with it, you believe with it, you act with it. When it hurts, you hurt. When it is caressed, you are caressed. ". . . I am my body. . . ." Let this be an unhurried meditation on your "bodiedness."

Now switch your statement to "I am *not* my body, I am *not* my body . . ." Continue to look at yourself in the mirror, but feel your independence from your body. You are not its weakness. Your being is not defined by its lines. You are more than a few dollars' worth of raw materials. You are memory and anticipations. You are imagination, taking you where your body cannot go. You are relationships. You are what you love and feel, hope and fear. ". . . I am not my body . . . I am myself." Let this be an unhurried meditation on your transcendence of your body.

■

Could you do this? Did you prefer meditating on your unity with, or your separateness from, your body? Feeling more or less alienated from our bodies is a part of being human. It is probably part of our rational nature to be observers of ourselves. This produces distance, even strangeness. However, our culture also encourages distance from our bodies. You may have had great difficulty appreciating your body if you looked at it with someone else's eyes. Most of us, perhaps women more than men, are conditioned to see ourselves as we think we would be approved or disapproved of by someone else. Our cultural stereotype of physical beauty robs us of self-appreciation. We give away our eyes, seeing the world and ourselves through others' eyes, prescribed for us like a pair of poorly fitted glasses. We allow ourselves to be sold a romantic ideal of beauty, with all the flesh placed in exactly the right proportions in the right places, with no awkward bumps, lumps, lines, or blemishes. We believe the ads for reforming ourselves in the image of a department store manikin. Thus, we lace ourselves into shapes as restricting as any Victorian corset, often ignoring the realities of biology or emotional health.

Yet it is possible to alter your relationship with your body. You can reject an unrealistic and idealized cultural image of how a body ought to look. Think what an uninteresting and unviable race we would be if we actually succeeded in reshaping ourselves to any ideal, no matter how perfect! Uniqueness and individuality are among our most precious possessions.

It can also be useful to experience self-touch separately from self-sight. We have some cultural stereotypes about how a body should feel. There is the "skin as soft as silk" fantasy. But the touch of a hand against a face is not completely victimized by the ideal. You may have had an experience like this: "I just came from the bedside of my aged mother, who is dying. I sat by her side for an hour with the back of my hand held lightly against her cheek. Before my eyes was her shrunken, wizened body, but my touch felt the incredible softness and loveliness or her skin against mine." Beauty can be available to one of our senses while it is clouded to another. Touch may feel what our eyes cannot see.

To experience your own skin, not as an obsession with yourself but as a means of self-discovery, can be well worth a few moments' exploration. Flesh may be flabby or firm and still be pleasant to touch. The difference is that soft flesh is enjoyed by soft touch, and firm flesh is enjoyed by a firmness of touch that meets its firmness. If you have a double chin, feel how pleasant it can be to touch gently. If you grab it too firmly, it presents itself as flabby rather than soft. By contrast, touch the firm muscle of your arm or leg. Unless you grasp it firmly, you will have only pleasant contact with the skin. You will not feel the muscle with its firmness and strength.

> Sketch a front view of yourself. Do not worry about your artistry. Let happen whatever will. When you have finished, place plus signs on the parts of your body you are comfortable touching. Put several pluses on the places you enjoy touching most. Place minus signs on any spots you are uncomfortable touching. Put several minus signs on those spots you strongly dislike touching.
>
> Test out the accuracy of your marks the next time you take a bath or shower. Do you enjoy rubbing warm soapy water on all parts of your body, or on some parts more than others? Do you rub with your hands alone, or are you more comfortable with a washcloth between your hand and your skin? How would you revise your picture in the light of this experience?

This exercise may reveal some anxieties and personal turmoil. It may show that you are uncomfortable with self-touch or have difficulty with touch in general. It can, however, suggest that there are other ways of experiencing yourself.

Self-acceptance is some kind of balance between alienation from self, on the one hand, and narcissism, on the other. In that middle range there are many choices that will be the product of values tested and affirmed. Self-hatred, including hatred of your own body, may be a disease requiring medical healing, but a milder lack of self-acceptance is a disability from which we all suffer to a lesser or greater extent. You may have feelings and attitudes toward your body that are deeply ingrained and difficult to manage, but it is not necessary to be victimized by them. Within limits you can choose ways of behaving that will allow you to value your body and self-pleasure more—if you so desire.

Whether or not masturbation is part of your sexual style, the ability and willingness to experience pleasure from your body may be important to other values you wish to choose. Willingness to accept and affirm yourself and your body is related to the desire and ability to affirm other people. Among the more important value choices you make are those by which you balance self-concern with concern for others.

Here too our culture has given us conflicting messages. On the one hand, you are told, "Take care of yourself. You can't expect others to do it for you." On the other hand, you are told, "Don't be selfish; be kind and generous. Always look after the other person." When these messages are translated into sexual terms, they say, "Don't expect your lover to give you pleasure." But, "It's up to you to give your lover a good time." This is a no-win situation. Where do you come in? No wonder you feel cheated. And nobody feeling cheated makes a great lover.

Taking Care of Yourself

Now we come to the act of masturbation itself. You are alone. The music is playing softly. The lights are dimmed. A breath of incense is wafting through the air. Before you is a bed piled with pillows and spread with silky sheets. A stack of sex magazines sits on the bedside table. An array of vibrators, dildoes, feathers, rings, jellies, lotions, and potions are scattered on the shelves around the bed. You have all the time necessary to please yourself sexually. Submerge yourself in the experience.

Do you want to escape as quickly as possible or try every aid available? If you might enjoy it, spend a few moments daydreaming about what you would do, how you might pleasure yourself.

If you wanted to escape this room as quickly as possible, you probably have some deep-seated feelings that masturbation is wrong, "sick," or dangerous. Solo sex may not be for you, even if you have changed your intellectual judgments about it. You might try saying, "Solo sex is fine for some people, but it's not a value for me. And that's okay." How does it feel when you say that?

If you remained in the room, did you use any of the mechanical or chemical aids? You may find these very exciting and stimulating, or you may feel they add to whatever feelings you already have about masturbation depersonalizing sex. Lotions and potions may trigger feelings of sexual arousal or feelings of slimy nastiness, or both.*

As you considered masturbating in the room of sexual pleasures, did any of the following thoughts occur to you?

1. "I could really enjoy myself in a place like this if no one knew I was doing it."

2. "This would be fine if I didn't have a sexual partner, or if my partner were away for some time. But I do have an available partner, so it doesn't seem quite right to be here."

3. "This is great for me, but I certainly wouldn't want my partner to wander into a similar room. There are so many satisfactions available here, I'd never be approached for intercourse again!"

4. "How I wish my partner could be here! We could have a great time playing around with all these things, both separately and together."

5. "It would be fun to come here now and again, but solo sex could never take the place of interpersonal sex for me."

Did you think that you could really be happy in the room of sexual pleasure only if your partner was also there? For many people, hand-genital play is an important part of their foreplay or lovemaking style. In fact, fears about masturbation may reduce one's capacity to enjoy sex play in general. What is commonly called mutual masturbation can be a couple's major expression of their involvement in, and pleasure with, one another. It is definitely not solo sex. *Mutual pleasuring* might be a better term for this type of interpersonal genital contact. You may greatly enjoy this kind of activity and still find solo sex unappealing.

Alternatively, did you think that you could enjoy this room alone—at

---

* Whatever your feelings are, it should be remembered that aids should be used with care. Lotions can cause rashes or other allergic reactions in some people. It is possible to infect or disturb the chemical balance of the vagina, and nothing should ever be introduced into the vagina unless it is medically approved for such use. Dildoes (simulated penises, usually made of plastic) appear to be harmless, but care should be taken in inserting them so as not to bruise or perforate the delicate tissues of the vagina. Vibrators are the subject of some controversy among users and experts. It is a fact that the male penis is no match for a vibrator in the effectiveness of clitoral stimulation. But then, the penis cannot really compete with the dexterity of a hand. Any "competition" can be won by the penis only because of the psychic and interpersonal factors that surround intercourse. Some sexologists therefore recommend against the use of vibrators; they feel the stronger stimulation may impede the development of the psychic factors necessary for orgasmic interpersonal sex. Other sexologists, however, believe this attitude expresses a moral bias about how sex should be rather than a sexological judgment. They feel the vibrator is simply a means to more certain orgasm for many women.

least, under some circumstances? Perhaps you feel good about masturbation, providing it is really private. Dealing with others' fears and judgments is what upsets you. Maybe you feel comfortable masturbating providing you have a "good" reason to do so. These reasons could be anything from no partner or an absent partner to an inability to get the sexual satisfactions you desire from your partner.

These "good" reasons that people use to justify solo sex, however, are sometimes two-edged swords. Suppose your spouse or lover said, "I want to masturbate just to add a bit of spice to our already terrific sex life." What do you feel? Now suppose he or she changed the message to "I need to masturbate because you never give me the sexual pleasures I want." Now what do you feel? Did your stomach tighten or the anger rise in your throat at the second statement? Obviously a partner can make masturbation a very threatening activity indeed.

Like all sexual activities, masturbation has many meanings. It is not so much the activity, but the value put on that activity, that is the primary choice. Some choose not to value solo sex in their sexual style. Others choose to explore the creative possibilities of solo sex along with interpersonal sex. A few choose to use it destructively. For still others, who follow different goals and values, the choice is solo sex or no sex at all.

5

Just Sex, Please:
The Casual Style

Sex with no strings attached. No fuss, no bother—nothing required beyond mutual attraction and willingness. Is this the ultimate in sexual pleasure, or is it the road to ruin? In this chapter we will be exploring the values involved in pursuing a sexual style that asks for little or no relationship between the sexual partners.

Casual sex is our term for sexual encounters that by circumstance or choice are occasional, impromptu, or incidental—that is, sex that is separated from love and may even be separated from acquaintance. Here there is no ongoing relationship requiring emotional attachment, and no commitment is made or expected. If a relationship is maintained with a sexual partner over time, it is for the express purpose of physical pleasure and sexual satisfaction: "He's great in bed, but I don't know what we'd ever talk about if we had to live with each other." The emphasis is on the sexual nature of the encounter.

Have you ever had a casual sexual encounter, anything from a "once in a lifetime" fling to an ongoing "only sex and nothing more" relationship, from a single furtive visit to a prostitute to a series of "one-night stands"? Are such encounters a regular part of your sexual behavior, or did you say after one or two of these experiences, "No—that's not for me"? Do you still engage in casual sex occasionally as you try to sort out what is important to you sexually?

The sex experts are not likely to proclaim that casual sex is or is not good. At the moment there is no simple answer. For example, sex therapist Helen Singer Kaplan writes, "Some men and women function best sexually with a variety of partners or with partners with whom they have limited relationships or who are emotionally unavailable." However, she goes on to state her clinical opinion that "a feeling of love between partners makes sex an infinitely more satisfying, pleasurable and human experience."[1] Masters and Johnson take a position generally supporting the importance of relationship in sexual satisfaction. Nevertheless, they write, "Sex and love are separate life forces, each capable of being sustained without the other."[2] For the time being, at least, you are thrown back on your own values in choosing between casual and relational styles.

Sampling the Sexual Smorgasbord

What are your images of casual sex? A jet-set romance, a "quickie" in a seedy brothel, a convention fling, the Thursday-luncheon rendezvous, a pickup from a singles bar? Does it seem exciting and fun, or dreary and dehumanizing? Think about the words *casual sex*. Say them aloud several times, in several tones of voice. The images that pop into your head could surprise you. Casual sex is one of those very emotive subjects on which we often suppress negative feelings if we think we are "liberated," or we suppress positive feelings if we "know" it is bad.

Probably the most common image of casual sex is the one-night stand: picking somebody up somewhere, somehow; having sex; then disappearing into the darkness. Henry is an engaging man in his early fifties. He is warm and intelligent and has several deep, enduring friendships. However, for most of his life he has been completely casual sexually. He has had sex with more than three thousand different people. But none of his enduring friends, including the person he lives with, has been a sexual partner. For Henry, mixing sex with friendship is a recipe for disaster. Every time he has ventured to have sex with a person who was important to him, the relationship has turned sour. He now sticks strictly to the one-night stand —having sex with like-minded casuals wherever he can find them.

If your first reaction to Henry is, "Ridiculous! No one can have had sex with that many people!"—then look again. Henry is real. In fact, we have had more than one Henry confide in us, and none of them has been a prostitute.

Oftentimes people try to ignore behaviors that they don't think they should like but are secretly attracted to, or behaviors that they think they should tolerate but basically find repulsive. How do you react to Henry? Is it stimulating to imagine so many sexual partners? Is the adventure and risk that might be involved in such a style enticing? Or do you feel slightly nauseated by Henry's style? Do you think he is doing the best he can with his own incapacity to deal with human relationships? Or do you feel cer-

tain he is too easily trading the satisfactions of significant sexual relationships for a sexual "flea market"?

If you find Henry's style to be distasteful, this need not mean that you
would find all casual styles to be distasteful. Here are some young people
pursuing other varieties of casual sex:

Mark avoids relationships of any depth, but he wants a regular sex life.
He doesn't like "just sleeping around," because finding new partners takes
too much time and energy. Besides, he finds sex to be more enjoyable
when he and his partner have been together a few times. Several months
ago Mark met Helen at a party. He asked her out, and they had a really
good time. As he usually does, Mark frankly told Helen that while he
found her attractive and wanted her sexually, she should know that "that
is as far as it will go." Helen laughed at that and teased him about being
so conceited that he thought every woman was about to fall in love with
him. Toward the end of the evening they wrestled and tumbled on
Helen's bed. She pretended to be a beauty queen and he a wrestler, each
of them strutting around the room. Then she playfully accused him of
being all show and demanded to see if he was really a man. He unzipped
his fly, revealing a very erect penis. More antics ensued, and they ended
the evening with intercourse.

After this Mark and Helen met regularly to exchange sex and light-
hearted banter. As the weeks went by, however, Helen became tender and
even solicitous of Mark. He began to worry about their relationship "getting serious." One evening he told Helen about his anxiety and asked her
to join him in getting things back to a just-sex basis. She responded that
she really did want a deeper relationship. Because sex is important to
her, she wants to know quite early in a relationship if sex is going to be
good. But in the end, sex alone is not very satisfying. This heart-to-heart
talk revealed that they wanted quite different things from being together.
Mark wanted sex with no future. Helen wanted sex as an exploration of
a possible future. Neither would supply what the other wanted.

Mark's next partner was Linda. They see each other about once a week,
and their attraction is almost exclusively sexual. Linda enjoys sex immensely, is very active sexually, masturbates frequently, and occasionally
goes to bed with someone she has just met, sometimes without ever
seeing him again. (She insists that the man wear a condom, and she has
frequent medical checkups. She knows these precautions against venereal
disease are not completely dependable, but she says, "Sure, I could get
killed in the bath, too, but I don't stop taking baths!") Mark has little
fear that Linda might fall in love with him, because her emotional investment is in Ted, who lives several hundred miles away. Linda and Ted see
each other for a long weekend every few weeks. They plan to marry in a

year or so. Meanwhile, both feel free to have sex with anyone they wish—no questions asked. They intend to keep this style after they are married, too.

How do you feel about these three people? Would you welcome any of them as friends or partners? First, what about Mark? Would you, or do you, enjoy his style of "only sex and nothing more" relationships? Do you think he is hurting other people with his style? Is he afraid of intimacy or responsibility? Or is he simply being realistic, recognizing that intimacy and commitment are not values for him? Would you like to spend some time with him, finding out more about his sexual style?

Next, what about Helen? Is she correct to want to check out sex early in a relationship? Was her experience with Mark just unfortunate, or do you think she needs some "good advice" about how to form lasting relationships. Do you think she deliberately deceived Mark, or was she simply pursuing her own understanding of how relationships grow? Is she hurting herself or others with her style? How do you like her style?

Finally, what about Linda? Does her sexual style appeal to you? Do you find her exciting and interesting, or do her freedom and sexual intensity make you uncomfortable? Is she taking big risks with her health and happiness? Or is she simply the kind of person who gets a lot of enjoyment out of life because she doesn't worry too much about tomorrow? Do you think she is going through a stage in her life and will "settle down" later, or has she chosen a permanent sexual style? Would you like to know more about Linda and her style?

If you are the least bit intrigued by any of these three life-styles, take three sheets of paper and place the name of one of the three persons at the top of each sheet. Put a line down the middle of each page, and in the left-hand column list every advantage you can think of for the sexual style that person has chosen. In the right-hand column list all the disadvantages that person is likely to encounter.

Then rank the advantages and disadvantages on a 1-to-3 scale. Give a 3 to items that are very important to you, a 2 to those that are somewhat important, and a 1 to those that make no difference to you. Which side ends up "carrying the most weight" for you in each case?

Finally, consider how sex and age may be influencing your evaluation:

1. Make Mark female (Martha), Helen male (Hal), and Linda male (Len). Would this change your list of advantages and disadvantages?

2. Imagine Mark, Helen, and Linda to be in their late forties. What would be different in your lists now? Do the styles become more or less appealing?

Now let's put some labels on these styles and look more closely at the specific ways a person may value casual sex.

Permanently casual. This is Mark's style, as well as Henry's. Both want sexual pleasure, but neither values personal intimacy, general companion-ship, depth, or affection in sexual relationships. These things are fairly easy for Henry to avoid with his one-night stands. But Mark sometimes has to work actively to avoid such involvements in his ongoing just-sex relationships. Not everybody who begins a relationship with sex wants to exclude other interpersonal values if the sexual relationship continues over time. It is also unlikely that a sexual style that is permanently and ex-clusively casual can fulfill the usual human needs for love and affection. However, this is equally true of a celibate style, and yet many people who choose this style function well as persons.

Who chooses a permanently casual style?

- People whose life situation or vocational purpose would make perma-nent relationships difficult or undesirable may prefer casual sex. We have known people working for a social cause or a large international charity who have chosen this style because they think it would be un-fair to inflict a permanent partner with their constant traveling and near complete involvement in their jobs. (Often they are not very expressive sexually, but when they have sex, it is casual sex.)
- People may choose this style because of the high value they place on freedom and variety. The freedom to have sex with anyone they please, any time they please, so long as the partner is willing, is an enticing notion.
- Most people who choose this style do so to avoid what they feel to be the disadvantages of relational sex. They want to avoid in their sex life the hassles, pain, and turmoil that intimacy and affection can sometimes bring.

Temporarily casual. This is Helen's style. For her, casual sex is not in-tended to be a permanent way of life. She enjoys sexual pleasure, but she is really looking for depth and duration in a relationship in which sex is only one of the more important elements. She does not value casual sexual contacts highly in themselves; they are primarily a means of exploring another person in the search for a permanently satisfying relationship. Here are some other people who have chosen to be temporarily casual:

- a college student, sexually active, but not wanting any involvements until education is finished;
- a young professional woman, feeling that anything more than casual sex would for the present get in the way of her career advancement;
- a divorcee, seeking confirmation that she is still sexually attractive;
- a divorced man, still angry with women, being sexually aggressive but avoiding intimacy;
- a young person "playing the field" in preparation for marriage;
- an elderly widower, still wanting sex but unable to dream of starting over with a new wife.

These people are all either "prerelational" or "postrelational." There are two quite different reasons for their choice of a temporarily casual style. Helen is using casual sex as an exploration of a relationship. The divorcee is using casual sex to explore her own sexual attractiveness. The young people are using it to explore sex itself. The casual sexual style of the others is seen as a temporary suspension of their preferred or normal style. They are more or less marking time by having casual sex. The college student and the young professional woman both expect to be relational in the future, when things have worked out. The widower may suspend what has been his normal style until death, or he may return to relational sex once he has finished grieving for his lost wife.

Of course, these people may be kidding themselves. The college student may turn out to be another Mark and never change his style. The divorced man may think he is just marking time when he is really getting back at women. The young person seeking to be sexually experienced may really be using this as a justification for "just having a good time." "This is only temporary" may mean "I haven't made up my mind about this."

Supplementarily casual. This is Linda's style. She has a primary relationship with Ted. It is there that her needs for intimacy and permanence are met. But she likes variety and excitement in sex; so she supplements her relationship with Ted with casual sexual contacts. She has her just-sex relationship with Mark, and she also enjoys an occasional fling with anybody who happens to attract her. Actually she could have supplemented her relationship to Ted with another sexual relationship of some depth and affection, but that would not have been casual. (The implications of a supplemented style for a primary relationship are discussed in Chapter 7.)

Supplementary casual sex also has wide variations in motivation. A person may genuinely desire sexual novelty and excitement or may wish to compensate for an unhappy sex life in a primary relationship. Outside casual sex may seem less threatening to a marriage than engaging in another significant sexual relationship. On the other hand, the casual sexual contacts may be used to punish or threaten the primary partner.

Casual behavior may involve one-night stands and sex with strangers, or it may be restricted to just-sex relationships of longer duration. It may be an essential part of a sexual style or happen only very rarely. In the latter case, it is pointless to talk about someone having a supplementarily casual *style*. Casual sex is not a sexual style unless acted on with some regularity and purpose. To say, "Same time, next year," would indicate a value but still not necessarily a style. For a happily married, normally monogamous person who nevertheless enjoys an annual sexcapade, casual sex is given such a low priority among life values that it would be inappropriate to say the person has a casual style. However, for a married person who says, "Same time, next year," to fifteen or twenty partners a year, casual sex is not just a low-priority value but a style of life. This person has a supplementarily casual style. The casual behavior is not a momentary departure from a more settled or essential sexual style.

If you indulge in casual sex, can you place yourself in one of these categories? Does casual sex supplement one or more significant sexual relationships for you, or are you exclusively casual? Do you think your current casual behavior is likely to be a permanent part of your style, or do you expect it to be different in the future? Check where you fit.

	Temporary phase	Permanent way of life
Exclusively casual		
Supplementarily casual		

The difference between being exclusively or supplementarily casual is one of behavior. You either have only casual contacts, or you also have an important relationship or two. The difference between a temporary and a permanent style, however, is mainly one of attitude. Actually, of course, people who intend their style to be permanent may at a later time move into a relationship that is not casual. Similarly, casual behavior intended to be temporary may turn out to be permanent. You can have casual affairs indefinitely in the belief that you are searching for something more than sex. You can wait a lifetime for circumstances to change. If you checked the "temporary" box, you might like to consider how long you have been in this temporary phase and realistically how long it is likely to continue.

How Casual Is Casual Sex?

By now you should have realized that there is a wide variety of sexual styles that can be grouped under the word *casual*. Many people have, now or in the past, included casual sex in their sexual styles. Probably very few of them, however, are as casual as our friend Henry. Most people who adopt a casual sexual style draw a line somewhere beyond which sex becomes permissible. Where do you draw this line? In the next few pages we will help you answer this question.

> Suppose you are married or have a steady relationship. You are at a convention in a distant city without your partner. You find yourself with a person to whom you are intensely attracted sexually, and you get a clear message from that person that you could go to bed together. It would be "just for fun." You are sure no one will ever know.
> Would you make the first move? Why or why not?
> What would you do or say if the other person made the first move?
> If you did sleep with this person and found yourself in his or her city a year or so later, would you try to make contact? Why or why not?

If you react less negatively toward this situation than to earlier examples, you may be willing to engage in casual sex occasionally but unwilling to adopt a casual style. "It's okay if it happens," you might say, "but searching out casual contacts is bound to get messy."

Next, how exactly do you manage direct sexual contact in relation to other forms of physical intimacy? Most people are willing to be casual about tennis or dancing, doing these things comfortably with a variety of partners. When it comes to hugging and kissing, a degree of relational discrimination may come in, until there are some activities that are reserved only for deep relationships. On the other hand, a person who is willing to have sexual intercourse with a stranger may never kiss that sexual partner and indeed limit kissing to persons with whom there is an important interpersonal relatedness.

> Here is a list of more and less sexually intense actions. Reorder the list, beginning with the action you regard as the *least* intimate or intense

sexually and ending with the action you regard as *most* intimate or intense.

Actions Listed Randomly	*Your Reordered List*	
Hugging	A.	Least intimate
Oral-genital contact	B.	
Holding hands	C.	
Hand-genital contact	D.	
Genital contact, intercourse	E.	
Kiss on the cheek	F.	
Kiss on the mouth	G.	
Facial caress	H.	
Upper-body caress	I.	
Lower-body caress	J.	Most intimate

Now ask yourself, "With whom, if anyone, have I been willing to do each of these things? Below are listed some categories of possible sexual contacts. Place the letter for each action (A, B, C, and so on, on your reordered list) next to every category of persons with whom you would be willing to do that action. You may wish to have particular people in mind as you do this. (We suggest that you do this exercise privately so that you can be more easily honest with yourself.)

1. A person with whom you are not at all acquainted

   _____

2. A person with whom you are only slightly acquainted

   _____

3. An attractive friend with whom you share common interests and enjoyments

   _____

4. A person with whom you have a relationship of great affection or love

   _____

5. A person with whom you have a committed relationship

   _____

Would you have filled in the letters in the same way five years ago? Would you like your pattern to be different five years from now?

You may have experienced some discomfort in doing this exercise if you needed to qualify your answers: "Well, under some circumstances I might do that, but under other circumstances, certainly not." So, how then do you choose a casual partner? You may be willing to have sex with anyone who also seems willing, no questions asked. On the other hand, you may look for a certain type of partner or a special set of circumstances.

Here are some possible qualifications for having casual sex:

- A prospective casual partner must be married or otherwise involved in another relationship.
- A prospective casual partner must be a realistic candidate for a fuller, more-than-sexual relationship.
- A prospective casual partner must be physically very attractive.
- It must be impossible for anyone to find out about the casual contact.
- There must be physical separation from a primary partner.

Are any of these qualifications yours? Make your own list of what you require in a casual sexual encounter.

These qualifications can reveal much about what is important to you or what you particularly fear or dislike. For example, some people limit casual contacts to persons who they know are already involved with someone else, because they believe such persons are less likely to make other demands. Other people avoid casual contact with anyone in an important relationship. This may be because of concern for the other's relationship, or it may be because of fear of the wrath of a jealous lover. Similarly, some people use casual sex as an exploration for a future relationship; so they want an unattached partner who seems a long-term prospect. Others avoid sexual relations with anyone who it seems the least bit likely may want sex with a future. What are the motives behind the various qualifications you have set down?

You can achieve a good deal of clarification about who you are sexually if you simply reflect on your social relationships. If you have tried the exercises here and searched your past experience for the insight it has to offer, you probably know by now whether you have chosen a casual style in order to avoid the disadvantages of relational sex or because of the advantages you see in the casual style itself. Are you happy with your choice, or is there some other style you might like to consider for the future?

The Art (or Artfulness) of Seduction

In casual sex the invitation to sexual encounter often comes quickly. People do not spend long hours, days, or months nurturing a relationship. Thus, the practice of seduction arises. One person artfully tries to entice another. A skillful seduction involves subtle bodily messages as well as tantalizingly ambiguous verbal messages. It becomes a game of skill, with ploy and counterploy, maneuver and countermaneuver.

People who value casual sex often defend their style by saying, "As long as no one gets hurt, there's nothing wrong with a just-sex relationship." But seduction games can hurt, and a person whose casual style presupposes sex without hurtful consequences should pay attention to the seduction game. In fact, it is essential that the game and the issues behind the game be understood both by those who don't wish to play and by those who do.

One traditional scenario goes like this: Dick is attracted to Jane. Jane is attracted to Dick. The possibility of affection between them must first run an obstacle course. Dick seeks to seduce Jane. If he does not try, he is not a man. If he does try, he is mischievous, but not really bad. If he succeeds, he can feel proud of his sexual powers, but alas, he has removed Jane from the list of "good girls" who might be appropriate objects of Dick's affection. If Jane resists, she remains on the list of good girls and Dick may or may not develop affection for her. If he doesn't, Jane does not know if it is because she has refused him and he regards her as a cold fish. If Jane resists, Dick doesn't know whether she has refused him because she doesn't like him or because she is "good." If Jane does succumb to Dick's seduction, he doesn't know whether it is because she likes him or because she is "that kind of girl." Then if he doesn't like her, he may tell his friends that she is "that kind of girl." If he tells them, then she is removed from the list of good girls who are appropriate objects of affection for anyone who hears the story. Of course, Dick and Jane cannot discuss any of this directly but engage in various ploys, trying to find out what they need to know without asking.

If this old scenario is falling out of fashion, there are new ones to take its place. How about this one: Dick is attracted to Jane. Jane is attracted to Dick. Dick thinks that if he tries to seduce Jane, she will think he is only interested in her body. But he is afraid that if he doesn't try to seduce her, she will think, (a) "He doesn't like me," or (b) "He is 'square,' dull, not 'hip' "—whatever. If Dick does try to seduce Jane, she may think, "He is a 'hip' kind of guy who goes to bed with anybody, and he is not doing this because he is attracted to me." So what happens? Answer: (a) nothing, and each thinks the other doesn't like him/her, or (*b*) something, and each thinks the other is interested only in bodies and sex. The new scenario ends like the old one: Dick and Jane do not discuss any of this but engage in all kinds of ploys, trying to find out what they wish to know.

Here is another up-to-date scenario: Dick is attracted . . . and so on. Dick is afraid to try to seduce Jane because she might reject him. Even if she doesn't, she may be having sex with him just because she is liberated and will do it with anybody. So he decides to seduce her by playing the game of "liberation." He tells her he knows she is a liberated woman, and since he is liberated too, they can have sex and it won't mean anything. So, (*a*) they have sex, and sure enough, it doesn't mean anything, or (*b*) she turns him down, and that shows him that she doesn't like him and that she is not liberated. They talk, but it is about what *isn't* going on between them.

> You may find it useful to examine some seduction scenarios in which you personally have been involved. Choose some sequence of events in which you were part of a game of seduction. Write out or replay in your mind the events that took place. It may be helpful to exaggerate or caricature the game that was played, in order to see the important features of the interaction. What were the initiating ploy, the responsive move, the resulting action, and the emotional resolution? How could you have played the game differently to avoid misunderstanding?

A fascinating and revealing aspect of seductive games is the fact that they tend to move back and forth across the boundary between fantasy and reality. Flirting and making suggestive comments are often only half serious. If the ploy doesn't work, you can fall back on being playful and unserious. If it does work, then you have to make a choice whether to be serious or not. Seductive encounters are often unserious from the beginning and remain so. We come close to living out our fantasies by playing in conversation and bodily contacts as if we were going to act out sexually, when in fact both persons are clear that this is not going to happen.

This can be fun. It can also hurt. Frequently the players remain confused about the reality behind the game. It may be a way of propositioning someone by putting the risk entirely on the other person. Both sexual games and casual sex can be ways of seeking safety. Kidding around may ensure against actual contact or rejection.

How do you experience yourself as a participant in sexual ploys? Here is a way in which you can reflect on your role in developing sexual contacts.

With whom have you had sexual relations? (If you have had a number of partners with whom you have had genital sex, list these people; if you have had few or no such experiences, do this exercise using the names of people with whom you have had the most erotic contact or sexual feeling.) Either concentrate on the recent past, or go as far back in your memory as you wish. Working in privacy, make your list, and then mark each name with one or more of the following letters:

Place an *I* before the names of contacts that you *initiated*.

Place an *O* before the names of contacts that the *other* person initiated.

Place an *M* before the names of those who, you felt, *manipulated* you or pushed you into sex.

Place a *P* before those whom, you feel, you manipulated or *pushed* into sex.

Place an *R* before the names of those with whom you had a *relationship* of some depth or affection.

Place an *S* before those with whom the experience was pleasant or *satisfying* for you.

What patterns emerge? Are you always the initiator of these contacts, or do you usually fall in with someone else's wishes? Do you sometimes or regularly feel pushed into sexual relationships, or do you prod others into sex? Have all your sexual encounters been satisfying or not? If not, what leaves you with a bitter taste: feelings of being manipulated, lack of a deeper relationship?

Perhaps you already know all this about yourself. On the other hand, you may find some surprises in your patterns. We have found that women often receive important insight from this exercise because it reveals how much they have been trained to behave as subjects of other people's initiation. If you find yourself conforming to that cultural pattern, the question is whether you are comfortable with it, and further, whether there are any changes you might realistically expect of yourself if you do not like the way it is.

Perhaps while doing this exercise you discovered that there has been a change in your behavior over the years. You have learned how to resist a seductive ploy when you want to and to end up in bed when you want to. If so, good. You are a person now who can choose to be or not to be casual.

6

Sex with Love:
The Relational Style

Imagine yourself alone, utterly alone. You are who you are, but you exist in empty space. No one is present to you, not even in your imagination. Think about it. It is quite impossible even to imagine, isn't it? You are who you are in relation to other people and places.

Now, try imagining yourself completely without an identity of your own. You have no name. You are not separate in any way from anybody or anything. You have no beginning and no end. There is no "me" and no "not me." Absurd, isn't it? You are who you are because you are not what you are not.

The human spirit seems to be impelled by a movement toward separation: "I have a separate identity that is mine and mine alone." At the same time, it is impelled by another, almost opposite movement toward union: "I am in the world and I am involved in relationships with other people. I share a common life." To be more a separate individual is to be less a member of the whole. To be more dependent upon a group is to be less unique and distinct from the whole. These two tendencies are in tension, and yet human well-being seems to require both. People need to feel that they are different from others, separate and independent, not lost in some amorphous mass of humanity. On the other hand, they abhor isolation and loneliness and long to overcome alienation and be united with others, intimately and deeply.

There is mystery here. In order to participate in this union and intimacy with others, I must bring a sense of my separate identity. Yet I cannot achieve an identity of my own without participating in union in a life process that I did not create and that is there before me as a gift.

We experience ourselves as sexual persons in this same way. You have a sexual identity. You are a separate body, with boundaries and unique characteristics. You have an image of yourself as sexual, with feelings, needs, and desires that are exclusively yours. Yet this sexual identity is most meaningful in relationship to other human beings. You are drawn toward sexual union by a desire to overcome separation and aloneness and to mingle your being with that of another. Your separate identity is realized while it is being overcome in the union.

All sexual encounters, whether casual or relational, share this mysterious tension. In casual encounters there is greater separation, the fuller identity of the partners remaining outside the sexual relation. Accordingly, there is less participation of the wholeness of the persons in the sexual union. By contrast, in the sexual experiences of a relational style, there is less separation; the identities of the partners mingle in the union. There tends to be an accordingly greater participation of the wholeness of the persons in the sexual union. Thus, in casual sex, the need for separation can be richly satisfied, because sex does not involve the relational qualities of union. Sex and love are separated. In relational sexual styles, sex is expected to provide the emotional need for participation in a profound union. Love and sex go together.

There is more than one relational style, with greater or less emphasis on participation in the union. In the *total style*, the emphasis is upon a single union. Two people seek to invest their emotional energy exclusively in each other, including of course their sexual energy. Although this style places little emphasis on separation or independence, there is nevertheless a separate identity of the two people. The important point is that love and sex are inseparable, under any and all circumstances. In the *supplemented style*, the emotional need for union is provided in one primary relationship, while secondary sexual encounters, either casual or relational, satisfy a further need for separation. Love and sex are both required, but they are separable.

This and the following two chapters are devoted to the various styles of relational sex. In them we make great use of the words *love* and *affection*. Different people assign different behaviors as well as different feelings to these words, and you should think about what they mean to you. For someone engaged in a seductive ploy, "I love you" translates to "I want your body." For some people *love* is a shorter word for *affection*. A young woman lamented to us, "He doesn't love me." He defended himself: "I do too love you; I have a lot of affection for you." The difference was immediately obvious to both of them. For other people, love involves not only great affection but also mutual sacrifice, vulnerability, care, and respect.

> What do you mean when you say, "I love you"?
> _____ I like you.
> _____ I like being around you.
> _____ I have a lot of affection for you.
> _____ I want to spend the rest of my life with you.
> _____ I want our lives to interweave.
> _____ I am willing to have you make demands on me.
> _____ I am willing to sacrifice a great deal for you.
> _____ I want to take care of you.
> _____ I want you to take care of me.
> _____ I am willing to surrender control to you.
> _____ I am willing to let you see my imperfections.
> _____ I trust you to treat me with respect.
> _____ I accept you in your imperfectness.

Check all the statements that are included in your meaning of *love*. Add any others that you feel should be here. What you mean and what a partner means by *love* may be different. Within limits, the word *love* can mean what you and your partner want it to mean, providing you explore together the color and tone it takes on in your relationship. It will be useful, therefore, to do this exercise with your partner in order to check out how your understandings compare.*

Love Is an Aphrodisiac

For people who have a relational style, sex and love belong together. This point of view is spelled out in three basic beliefs. Let's examine them one at a time.

---

* Obviously, other words and phrases can contain a range of meanings. We will return to the problems these variations of word meaning can create in a later discussion of communications (Chapter 12). Meanwhile, if you find some word we are using to be rather vague, make your own list of possible meanings and sort through them as you have just done.

The more affection, the more sexual satisfaction. Helen Singer Kaplan writes, "Love is the only real aphrodisiac."[1] Among people who choose a relational style, there is a basic belief that affection is necessary to good sex. This may be simply a question of taste or preference: "I find that sex is better when I like my sexual partner as a person." Or it may be a matter of principle: "Sex outside a committed love relationship is wrong."

Below are some significant milestones in the development of a relationship. At which milestone do you feel sexual intercourse or genital contact becomes an appropriate or permissible expression of the relationship?

It becomes appropriate when the other person and I:

_____ are physically attracted to each other.

_____ clearly like each other.

_____ have developed a special friendship.

_____ have become the most important persons in each other's lives.

_____ have acknowledged that our relationship may have a future.

_____ have decided to maintain the relationship in the foreseeable future.

_____ intend to marry.

_____ have sealed our love with marriage vows.

If you feel intercourse or genital contact becomes appropriate at some point not mentioned here, write out and insert your personal milestone where it belongs in the list. Then mark at what milestone sex becomes *satisfying* for you. Is there a difference? Is your actual sexual behavior consistent with one or other of these markings?

Obviously, the farther down the list you place yourself in both thought and action, the deeper and more committed a relationship you want before having sex. The first milestone reflects a casual view of sex. The second one might indicate a relational or casual style—depending on how you define *like*. By the third milestone affection clearly exists in more than a sexual context. Reserving sex for these relationships or deeper ones indicates a belief in relational sex.

You may have found that sex is permissible for you at one milestone but satisfying only at another. Which milestone is reflected in your sexual behavior? For example, you may feel that sex is okay for any two people who are attracted to each other, but that sex is just "blah" for you personally until there is a special friendship. Or you might say that sex is appropriate only when two people intend to marry, but you actually have satisfying sex whenever there is a mutual attraction between you and another person. Looking at your behavior, you may find that you are following different standards in different circumstances. If so, can you say whether you act primarily on the basis of one style or the other?

The relational style claims that it is difficult to have good sex devoid of any other personal relationship. The new sex therapies indicate that to objectify sex is to invite difficulty in sexual functioning. There is no such thing as *the* perfect orgasm. Practice or sheer determination does not ensure peak orgasms. You cannot achieve the heights of sexual ecstasy in the same way you might train to clear fifteen feet in the pole vault. If your sexual style is relational, you interpret this to mean that sex should be kept within the context of a larger relationship. To compartmentalize sex is the beginning of objectifying it. The person who wants only relational sex believes that only within a broad, deep relationship can the full meaning and pleasure of sex be realized. The love, care, concern, mutual respect, intimacy, and trust transform *sex* into *lovemaking*. They make "the usual" feel extraordinary.

The more sexual satisfaction, the more affection. Sex reinforces love, as well as the other way around. The relational person, then, will turn Kaplan's statement around and say as well, "Sex is an 'aphrodisiac' for love." Good sex can make a good relationship better. It may even transform a dull relationship into one of enduring affection. The interaction between love and sex can produce an ever-increasing spiral of personal and physical union. A satisfying sexual relationship can influence the overall relationship of two people for the better. If sex is very fulfilling, it is apt to make other aspects of a relationship seem good—or at least bearable. How do you react to these ideas?

Think back over a significant relationship that involved sexual activity. Did the satisfaction you secured from sex ever smooth over other problems? Is that what made it worthwhile staying in?

Was sex so good that the understanding you reached in intercourse helped you to reach understanding in other areas of your life together? Did you ever end a good quarrel with intercourse? Did you ever feel that sex was especially good after a fight? On the other hand, did frustrating sexual experiences make the overall relationship worse, so that you began having difficulties in other areas as well? Or were other areas of your relationship unaffected by your sexual problems?

In short, what influence did sex have on the larger relationship? Did it help, harm, or have no effect at all? Did you keep your sex life quite separate from the rest of your relating? What does this experience tell you about your view of sex and relationship?

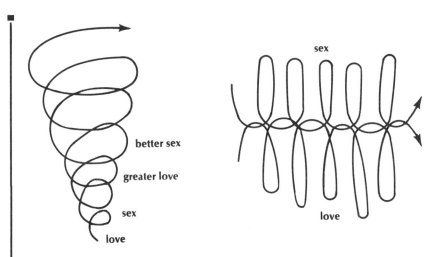

These are two pictures of how love and sex might relate to each other. In the one on the left, the better the sex, the more the love, and the more the love, the better the sex. In the one on the right, love and sex simply intersect regularly, perhaps supporting each other at that point but otherwise functioning independently. Does either picture fit your experience? If not, draw your own picture of the relationship between love and sex.

Sex is interpersonal communication. All these relational beliefs can be summed up: sex is a means of expressing the mutual care, esteem, and love present in a relationship. It can say what can be said in no other way. To separate sexual intercourse from its expressive function is to reduce it to biology. If these are your sentiments, then relational sex is your style.

If sex is a means of communication, it can be used to send a variety of messages. It may whisper sweet nothings into the ear of a lover, or it may say, "Drop dead, you klutz!" The man who is always "too tired" to have sex may be using this to get back at his wife for making so many demands on him. The woman who does not reach orgasm may be trying to keep control this way because she feels powerless otherwise in her relationship. Many sex therapists feel that too great a level of hostility in a relationship can make a sexual dysfunction virtually impossible to treat.[2] The couple must have enough goodwill to be willing to work on the problems together without sabotaging each other's progress.

This does not mean that couples who fight will have sexual problems. There are some sexologists who believe that a certain amount of aggression is necessary for exciting sex.[3] If a couple become too companionable, then their sex life is apt to become rather easygoing and companionable, too— and not very exciting. Some marriage counselors believe that a good, fair fight can lead to growth for both people and for their relationship. Fighting becomes destructive when it is constant and when it focuses on destroying the self-image of the partners rather than on managing the issues in conflict.

How does interpersonal relationship affect your sexual satisfaction? Following are some bar graphs listing, on the right, needs that people frequently wish to have met in ongoing relationships and, on the left, a contrasting situation, the negative consequence of these needs being absent or unmet.

To what extent must you have these needs met in a relationship in order to experience "great sex"—that is, sex that is highly satisfying and pleasurable for you? Can you have too much of one of these good things? Does a little hostility or even disrespect give zest to sex?

Black in the area of each bar that represents the spread you can tolerate in having that need met or not met and still experience great sex. Where between having that need met and having it unmet does the best sex come for you?

Crosshatch the area to the left and/or to the right that represents the mix of met and unmet needs that lets you experience "okay sex"— that is, sex that is satisfying but not particularly exciting.

Leave blank the part of each bar that represents unsatisfying sex.

If any graph is irrelevant to your experience of satisfying sex, then omit it.

There is a space to add other needs if you wish.

For example, a person who feels that too much security takes some of the spice out of sex, but who still needs some security to experience satisfying sex, might fill out the security graph like this:

Need not met					Need completely met
	Unsatisfying sex	Okay sex	Great sex	Okay sex	

Or a person whose security needs are very high might fill it in this way:

Need not met   **Need completely met**

Mistrust		Trust

Distance		Intimacy

Insecurity		Security

Hostility		Love

Selfishness		Mutual concern

Disrespect		Respect

Secrecy		Openness

Other		Other

If you found most of these items to be irrelevant to your experience of sexual satisfaction, then relational values are not important to you. If you found it impossible to rate "great sex," it may be that you prefer casual sex or that your style is nonexpressive. In studying these graphs, you may notice one or two needs that are quite essential to you in order to experience great sex. Are you pursuing a sexual style that values the needs that are most important to you?

Variations on the Relational Theme

Nancy and Gary met while they were at college and soon developed an affection for each other. They proceeded cautiously toward deeper levels of commitment, wanting to be sure of their feelings. When at length they became engaged, they considered having intercourse. Most of their friends were having sex and seemed to assume that they were too. After much discussion, they decided they would wait until they were married. To their surprise, this decision removed a lot of tension they had been experiencing. It clarified what turned out to be a basic belief for both of them— that intercourse should be reserved for the deepest commitment that two people can make to each other, "to love and to cherish, till death us do part."

Jason went to the same college but had quite different experiences. He felt that as soon as two people knew they liked each other, intercourse was okay. In fact, sex was a good way for two people to get to know each other better. He had friends whose company he enjoyed and whom it seemed natural to relate to sexually as well as socially. He did not expect these relationships to last a lifetime, and no one person yet fulfilled his criteria for a mate. As a group, however, they did satisfy most of his present emotional and sexual needs, and he found he was important in their lives as well.

Nancy and Gary clearly have a relational view of sexuality, but what about Jason? He got more out of these relationships than just sexual gratification. He believes he has a relational style. Do you agree? Obviously there is no clear-cut line between casual and relational sex. The difference is one of degree. People who pursue a relational style want more breadth and depth of relationship than do those who pursue casual styles. It seems highly unlikely that a one-night stand could be considered relational; little breadth or depth could be developed in that time span. But what about a sexual relationship that has lasted a month? If the couple have limited their relationship to sexual pleasuring, then they were clearly viewing sex casually. If, however, they develop a significant interaction in non-sexual activity and if they see sex as a natural expression of their affection, they then might consider themselves relational. The length of a relationship does not by itself determine whether it is casual or relational. Attitudes toward sex and toward the relationship may be important as well.

Relational people do not always agree on what it means to be relational. The differences center around two issues: duration and totality of relationship. How long a commitment must one person make to another? How total must this commitment be? The varieties of relational style emerge out of the different ways people answer these two questions. It is not fair yet to ask you how you answer these questions. You may have a general idea of how relational you want to be, but there are still some issues in relational sex you would need to explore further before deciding what you most appreciate. In the next two chapters we will be looking more closely at supplemented and total styles of relationship, providing a further opportunity to take the measure.

7

Sex with Love ... and Someone on the Side: The Supplemented Style

Sex that cannot be talked about cannot be organized into a system of cherished values. Traditionally, supplemented sex has been sex swept under the carpet. The secret affair, the furtive fling—these have been more often the subject of vigorous denial or locker-room humor than earnest dialogue. Only in recent years has the supplemented style of relational sex entered the public realm as a topic to be openly discussed and seriously considered. In this chapter we shall be exploring some of the advantages and difficulties in choosing a supplemented sexual style. What are the needs people seek to meet in having sex with more than one person? What are the pitfalls they may encounter and the satisfactions they may achieve in this pursuit?

First, let's get a bead on your own experience.

Think of the friends and acquaintances you encounter regularly and jot down the first fifteen or twenty names that come to mind. Looking at your list, do the following:

Cross off all those from whom you get no personal satisfaction. These are people you are thrown together with at work or whose paths cross your own of necessity.

Put a check by those from whom you get some social or intellectual satisfaction. You have some personal sharing with these people.

Circle those from whom you receive significant emotional satisfaction. You have some deep personal sharing with these people.

Underline any with whom you have genital sex, whether or not you have deep personal sharing with them.

If there are several names underlined but not checked or circled, this is a mark of casual sex. If there is one name, and only one, that is checked, circled, and underlined, all three, that is an indication of what we will call the *total style*, to be discussed in the next chapter. If there is at least one name checked, circled, and underlined but there are others underlined, that is a mark of the *supplemented style*. If no name is checked, circled, and underlined (all three), then you probably do not have a primary relationship to supplement. However, you may still be having relational sex if some person on your list is both underlined *and* either checked or circled.

Are you happy with the pattern that emerges on your list, or would you like it to be different? If different, would you like to get your sexual satisfaction from more or fewer people? If you receive most of your satisfaction from one person and are happy with this arrangement, then probably the supplemented style is not a serious consideration for you. If, however, you do, or might, enjoy sex with more than one person, then you will want to take a closer look at the supplemented style. If you are already pursuing a supplemented sexual style, you will want to confirm or modify your style in terms of the advantages and disadvantages you find in your exploration.

When Is More Better?

To those who conscientiously seek a supplemented style, the idea of two people trying to fulfill all of each other's needs appears unrealistic, if not ridiculous. To ask for deep emotional involvement, passionate sexual relations, stimulating intellectual interaction, and domestic tranquillity, all from one person, is to ask the impossible. Better to enjoy graciously what a partner can offer and seek further satisfaction elsewhere. To let a part of you wither for want of satisfaction or to pressure a partner to fulfill further needs is to invite disappointment and risk disruption of the relationship.

You may, of course, wish to supplement your primary relationship in nonsexual ways. In fact, most people do. You may have special friends with whom you share particular interests, perhaps recreational or cultural. You may frequent museums with Mary and go bowling with John. However, it is not easy in our society to have close friends of the opposite sex, especially when you are in a permanent relationship. If you are a married man, you do not frequent museums with a Mary, nor do you go bowling with a Joan—at least not without rejecting the traditional pattern. If you do, people will immediately wonder whether you are having sex with one or both of them.

There is a profound need in most of our lives for developing deeper, more meaningful relationships. Whether or not it is true that the old "extended family" provided for these wider intimacy needs, it is certain that we do not find them easily satisfied the way we organize intimacy today. Intermediate levels of intimacy are scarce. We know how to interact on a transactional basis, doing business at store, school, or office. There is such a paucity of intimacy, however, that when it becomes obvious that two people are interacting on a deeper level than "doing business," outsiders immediately assume that they are sexually involved. Many people, therefore, shy away from deep friendships in fear that they might turn sexual or even appear sexual. In a book about sex we obviously cannot deal comprehensively with this problem, but we can explore the limits you may wish to set on the physical expressions of affection in friendship.

Friendship is one thing, but what about sex? Surveys indicate that nearly half of all married Americans have an outside sexual relationship at one time or another in their married lives.[1] Mostly this sexual activity has been carried out secretly, without the knowledge of the spouse. These affairs are not usually the stuff from which sexual values are forged. People who "fall" into affairs or are "swept off their feet" have not reflected on the choices. Is it possible for the supplemented style to be a valued choice of sexual style?

The answer is, for some people, yes. The integrity of such a choice is easiest to see when there are some unusual circumstances to justify it. Here are some examples:

1. After Charles and Jane were married, Charles had a tragic accident that left him paralyzed and unable to satisfy Jane sexually. They have a wonderful relationship and have agreed that Jane can have sex with others.

2. Linda and Robert are separated for long periods. As an actress she is often away on location, while he remains behind at his medical practice. Both are very expressive sexually and feel that outside sex is permissible when they are separated.

3. Henry and May have teenage children. Apart from a long since evap-

orated sexual relationship, they are quite happy with each other and want to stay married for the children's sakes. They feel that discreet affairs will relieve sexual tension and strengthen their family life.

Each of these couples decided to permit outside sex, justifying that decision by their special circumstances. For others the same circumstances may work in quite an opposite way. We know one couple who used to have an "open marriage," each person having outside sexual relationships, until the husband's diabetes affected his sexual functioning. As a result, his wife feels it is unfair for her to "sleep around" when he cannot indulge in the same privilege. You personally may or may not agree that the circumstances in each case merit the decision the couple has made; but if they have considered the options and affirm their decision in action, then they value the supplemented style.

Obviously, most people who choose a supplemented sexual style do not do so as a result of unusual circumstances. Why can't two people involved in a happy relationship simply agree to let each other have significant outside relationships, including sexual activity? Can't marriage, or any committed relationship, be defined in a way that does not require sexual exclusivity? An increasing number of people answer yes. As one young woman put it, "Monogamy has been based on ownership of the other's body, especially the man owning the woman's body. My body is mine, not my husband's. It goes without saying that his body belongs to him. We *love* each other. We do not *own* each other."

The desire for personal and sexual freedom and the lure of novelty and variety provide strong motivations for the supplementary style. So does boredom, a major enemy of modern marriage. Perhaps in previous times people expected some drudgery and boredom in their lives. Present-day Americans do not; the creative, open, spontaneous person, gentle of others' feelings, but constantly popping up with new and exciting notions of where to go and what to do—this amounts to the image of a cultural hero. In exaggerated form it is a jet-set impresario. In more usual guise, it is the freewheeling guy at college, the vivacious gal at the office, the bon vivant, a connoisseur of both Art Nouveau and Chateaubriand. Partly this is chasing after rainbows. Partly it is authentic longing to explore the unknown, to be open to new experience, to leave behind the timid life that marches in rank order toward oblivion.

The supplemented style appeals most to persons with high independence and privacy needs. You may be committed to a model of growth that emphasizes the importance of intimacy and depth relationships to personal growth. To impose arbitrary limits on sexual relationships not only restricts one's independence but also may limit one's growth as a person. Outside sexual relationships can offer the opportunity for you to see yourself in new ways. Thus, the small costs may be worth tolerating or even affirming, rather than avoiding or hiding, because of the interpersonal satisfactions that are possible through a variety of relationships.

The person in the supplemented style may believe strongly in the autonomy of the individual. Each person in a relationship becomes "half a person" if each does only what both can agree upon. The only way two people can develop their full potential is to pursue their interests independently when they do not coincide. If outside sexual activity is seen as a desirable part of this personal fulfillment, then it will happen naturally.

Central to the supplemented style is a new definition of fidelity. Traditionally, fidelity has been defined physically. "He has been unfaithful to her" means he had intercourse with someone else. People who support the supplemented style redefine fidelity in terms of fundamental commitment rather than sexual exclusivity. The reasoning may go like this: "I must be faithful to myself if I am to be faithful to you. If I must violate my sense of what is right for me in order to please you, then sooner or later we both will suffer. This does not mean that I can selfishly do whatever I want. Exploiting or manipulating you for my ends would be a violation of both you and me. A loving concern for you, a willingness to make our relationship more important than any other relationship, is necessary. I offer love and receive love. I offer freedom and receive freedom. We agree to pursue faithfully the balance we have worked out between our individual needs and what is needed to make our relationship work."

How does this sound to you? Terrific—or utterly nonsensical? Realistic—or idealistic?

What do you mean when you say you are being "faithful"?

_____ I am being sexually exclusive.

_____ I am being true to myself.

_____ I show loving concern for my partner.

_____ I do whatever my partner wants.

_____ I provide my partner's physical or material wants.

_____ I would never dream of getting a divorce.

_____ Our relationship comes first, but it's not all there is.

Or does it mean something else to you?

Can you describe the balance you have worked out between your individual needs and your relational needs?

Do you give higher priority to individual or to relational needs?

To Talk or Not to Talk

The traditional affair involves secrecy rather than openness and honesty. People who advocate the supplemented style as an alternative to monogamous marriage often stress the importance of openness between the partners. If a couple are not going to accept the traditional definition of fidelity, then they need other ways to signify their primary commitment to each other. This requires that they speak frankly about their respective needs and how they are going to meet them, negotiating in trust with each other.

There is no doubt that good communication is important to the well-being of any relationship. The question then arises, Does *good* communication necessarily mean *more* communication? If two people have openly agreed that outside sex is okay, does that mean that they must tell each other every little detail about their outside sex life? We hear two main responses to this question: (1) "Yes; it's the relationship I don't know about that scares me." (2) "No; as long as I don't hear about it, I don't feel threatened." How do you react to this?

1. Imagine that you are in a sexually nonexclusive relationship. Your partner and you are comfortably discussing the day's events when your partner begins to describe in detail a lovemaking session with a lover: "And then for some crazy reason we got out the whipped cream and squirted it all over the right places. You know, just like they do in those porno films. It was fantastic! We licked and giggled. You and I really should do it sometime."

What would be your response?

a. "Gee, yes! Why not tonight?"

b. "Whipped cream? Yuk. I'd rather have lemon meringue."

c. "My God, if your lover thinks up exotic things like that, how much longer are you going to stick around with me?"

d. "Why don't you give me the sort of good time you give your lover?"

e. "Why can't you keep your escapades to yourself?"

f. "You pervert!"

Explore the threat or the thrill such an event would give you. Can you separate feelings aroused by the whipped cream from feelings caused by the partner's describing the lurid details?

2. Now imagine that you are in a relationship in which you have never really talked about whether you are to be sexually exclusive or not. Recently you have begun to notice that your partner is acting a little strangely—singing all the time and walking with a new bounce. In short, your partner just seems happier now than in a long, long time —and for no apparent reason. You are not normally a suspicious person, but gradually it begins to dawn on you that your partner might be having an affair.

What would you say or do?

    a. Ignore the situation.

    b. Do some sleuthing until you can confront your partner with the evidence.

    c. Ask your partner directly if he or she is having an affair.

    d. Tell your partner indirectly that you would disapprove of an affair.

    e. Tell your partner that if he or she is having an affair, you don't want to know about it.

    f. Tell your partner that you don't mind if he or she has an affair, but for goodness' sake, stop that awful singing!

    g. Tell your partner indirectly that you approve of his or her having an affair.

What do these two fantasies tell you about your view of openness? Is there a point at which you want to say, "No, I don't want to hear about it"? You may get a kick, even a sexual kick, out of hearing the lovely details, or you may have the threat reduced by knowing the details. On the other hand, telling all can be a potent weapon in relational conflicts. "We did this . . . and then we did that . . ." may translate to "You're a lousy lover," or something else equally devastating. The guise of openness may be used to seek revenge on a partner. Most of us are rather vulnerable when our sexuality is called into question.

The openness in "open marriage" is therefore not unlimited: "It's not the outside sex that's the problem; it's hearing about it that I can't handle." This has been a frequent refrain when an open marriage is being renegotiated in the aftermath of relational strain. These people have been searching for a style that would allow them to be sexually freer but that does not force constant discussion of supplementary relationships. That gets boring even when it is not threatening. These are not people pursuing the traditional secret affair. Rather they had agreed openly that it is to be expected that they will have other sexual relationships from time to time, but they will not report when or with whom. There is no "show and tell" time.

Partners who both have strong privacy needs may come and go as they please, no questions asked. Others may set aside one or two evenings a week when they are not expected to account for what they have been doing. Still others, who have strong intimacy needs, may agree that outside sexual activity can occur only at times when they would not be together anyway. Outside sex then remains invisible in the warp and woof of everyday life.

If openness can be a delicate matter, so can secrecy. Dave had an affair and confided in a good friend, "I can't tell Lucy—it would only hurt her. Besides, what harm does it do? I still love her." Gradually it became more difficult for him to maintain this secrecy without considerable deceit. He had to make up reasons for being away from home or to explain why he had not been at work when Lucy called. When keeping sexual secrets, it is frequently very difficult to sort out whether you are really protecting your partner or only avoiding unpleasant revelations.

Obviously it is more difficult to hide the ongoing affair than the sporadic casual sexual encounter. Since it is not possible to be in two places at once, tricks of magic may be required in order to maintain the secrecy of an arrangement that goes on week in and week out. Moreover, a spouse is much more likely to fear regular unexplained absences, such as Mondays and Thursdays, than some twice-a-year meeting of the Friends of the Crossbeaked Woodhatch. Secrecy about regular behavior almost inevitably leads to the practice of small deceits. The buildup of these dissimulations can lead to relational disaster. This does not mean that the sporadic sexual encounter is morally better. It does imply, however, that the consequences of secrecy are different in different situations and require careful consideration.

How Much More . . . of What . . . with Whom?

Let's assume the decision is made to have supplementary sex and that the question of how much openness has been settled. Now the burning question is, How much supplementation and of what kind? One extreme is, "Mary can have as deep a relationship to Jack as she wants. I don't care what they do—as long as they don't go to bed together. I couldn't take that." Someone else will say, "He can have the occasional sexual fling. That doesn't matter a darn to me, just so he doesn't get a regular thing going with somebody."

What freedoms would you be willing to give your partner? What actions would arouse feelings of betrayal in you if your partner did them without consulting you?

Below is a list of actions, both sexual and nonsexual, that your partner might do. Looking down the list, do the following:

Put a *P* next to those that you would feel comfortable having your *partner* do without your knowledge.

Put a *T* next to those you would like to *talk* about before your partner actually did them.

Put an *N* by those that you would *not* like your partner to do at all.

Assume in each case that the person involved is attractive to your partner.

( ) Have a regular night out with a group of the same sex.* ( )
( ) Go alone to a card game or music group that includes both sexes. ( )
( ) Get together regularly with one person of the opposite sex to pursue a common interest. ( )
( ) Go out to dinner with a person of the opposite sex. ( )
( ) Dance with other people at a party. ( )
( ) Kiss someone else at a party. ( )
( ) Dance with just one other person at a party. ( )
( ) Take someone else to the movies. ( )
( ) Pet heavily (hands on genitals) with someone else at a party or a movie. ( )
( ) Pet heavily with someone else in private. ( )
( ) Kiss someone else in private. ( )
( ) Do nude massage in a group with you present. ( )
( ) Do nude massage in private with someone else. ( )
( ) Have intercourse with someone else occasionally. ( )
( ) Engage in a group-sex party with you present. ( )
( ) Engage in a group-sex party without you present. ( )
( ) Have a long-term sexual partner other than yourself. ( )
( ) Have a close friend of the opposite sex and spend many hours each week with that friend without having intercourse. ( )

Now go back through the list and decide how much freedom you would like for yourself. Cover or ignore your coding for your partner. In the other space, place the following:

* People in same-sex relationships should read *opposite* for *same* in this exercise and *same* for *opposite*.

A *p* by those activities that you would like to be able to do without consulting your *partner*.

A *t* by those that you would want to *talk* about with your partner before doing.

An *n* by those that you feel you would *not* do at all.

Compare your two codes. Do you expect the same behavior of your partner that you expect of yourself, or are the expectations different? Are you more or less strict with yourself? Could you explain these differences to your partner, and would your partner understand?

If you are in a primary relationship, this will be a useful exercise to ask your partner to do as well. It can provide a framework for discussion of behavior that is independent of what you have been doing. You might use it to begin establishing an agreement about what you may or may not wish each other to do. Once again, do not compare codes until both of you have done the exercise. Activities that you and your partner code differently are the important ones to discuss. These are the ones that may arouse feelings of betrayal if one partner suddenly discovers them. If you feel reluctant to share this exercise with your partner, ask yourself why. Have you expected stricter behavior of your partner than you expect of yourself? Or do you fear that your partner expects stricter behavior of you than you wish to pursue?

Some people will make most of their judgments about the actions on this list in terms of moral rules. They will see some behavior as being permissible and other behavior as being wrong regardless of personal wishes. Some people will make their decisions on the basis of the reactions of third parties—children or society at large—and disapprove of behavior that is public while approving similar actions if they are private. Still other people will make their judgments on the basis of the threat each action poses to them. They will want to restrict their partner's behavior in activities that they fear may lead to the loss of affection. Accordingly, they may want to restrict their own behavior in order to hold a partner accountable to the same standards. Stability of relationship and personal security are then the important issues.

One far-out way of sexual supplementation is "swinging" and "mate-swapping." A couple agree to go to parties or meet other couples for the express purpose of exchanging sexual partners. Usually both partners are present, although not necessarily in the same room, when the sexual activity takes place. Moreover, married couples who swing usually limit their outside sexual activity to these couple encounters. The reasoning is that if partners can see the limited extent of the involvement, they will not be threatened by sex with someone else. There is nevertheless the excitement of a variety of partners and perhaps a further thrill from seeing or being near other people having sex. This combination of openness and casualness is intended to minimize the risks of outside sex, while providing variety, novelty, and excitement.

Swinging may be dramatic, but the most radical departure from traditional sexual styles is "group marriage." Three or more sexual partners enter into a long-term commitment to one another, perhaps even exchanging marriagelike vows. The group may be sexually exclusive, limiting sexual activity to those within the group marriage. In other cases, outside sexual liaisons are expected as a natural part of the rejection of traditional monogamy. The supporters of group marriage argue that the values of the old extended family, whether real or imagined, must be retrieved. Each member of the group has more than one person to turn to for both sexual satisfaction and other emotional supports. Group marriage is not always a highly expressive sexual style and in fact may be organized around non-sexual priorities.

Swinging and group marriage have received much publicity in recent years, but research indicates that they are quite rare.[2] The people who swing do not, by and large, depart otherwise from the typical values of the culture and keep their activities discreetly behind closed doors. It is most often the male partner who initiates the pattern but he is also more apt to be threatened and withdraw from it. The pattern tends to be temporary. Group marriage requires so great an expenditure of energy both to establish and to maintain that only people with very high commitment can bring it off at all. Not many people are willing to depart so drastically from the customs of society or to put the required energy into the marital relationship. Do you find group marriage attractive, if impractical? Do you find it unattractive? Why?

The central issue in the supplemented style is this: How can we have the freedom and spontaneity we wish in relating to other people and still have the intimacy and security we wish in our own relationship? This means that the way in which the partners succeed in managing the threat of outside relations is crucial. Little research has been done on what makes the supplemented style work for some people and not for others. One study of the married life of nearly five hundred successful, upper-middle-class Americans, many of whom did engage in sex outside the marital bond, was done by John Cuber and Peggy Haroff. They found that whether a couple was happy with this sexual style or not seemed to depend on (1) whether the partner knew about the outside relationship, (2) whether the partner agreed to it, (3) whether both participated in such behavior, and (4) whether agreement on the matter was genuine rather than forced.[3] In other words, "open" marriages seemed happier than those in which outside sex took place but was hidden.

It is sometimes tempting for the partner who wants more freedom to manipulate the situation in order to have what he or she wants. Some people urge their partners to have affairs so that they will feel less guilty about the affairs they are having or want to have. Another pattern is for a strong partner to tie the other up in dependency—emotional, financial, social—making the dependent partner helpless to prevent the stronger partner from doing what he or she likes. There are all sorts of ways, some subtle and some not so subtle, by which the person who wants greater freedom can pressure the other partner into accepting his or her behavior. Alternatively, the person who wants to restrict freedom can bring to bear all the weight of tradition and public morality, using them as cudgels to maintain a style of relationship highly destructive to a partner whose spirit strives for freedom.

Does the supplemented style have an appeal for you? Here are some questions to ponder as you consider it. There are alternate responses suggested, but formulate your own response.

Under what circumstances would you want to pursue this style?
> a. There would have to be some extraordinary circumstances, such as long illness or separation.
> b. Lack of complete sexual satisfaction is enough reason to seek outside sex.
> c. Desire for freedom and variety is enough reason to seek outside sex.
> d. It is natural to have outside sex with someone attractive and attracted.

What ground rules would you wish to follow?

On openness:
> a. We must talk about any outside sexual activity we have.
> b. Once we have agreed on what outside sexual behavior is acceptable, we do not have to talk about the matter again.
> c. No openness—we both do what we want but secretly, discreetly.
> d. We limit outside sexual activity to behavior that will not interfere with our normal routines together.
> e. We set aside certain times during the week for free and unrestricted activity.

   f. We have no limits on outside activity—we come and go with no
    questions asked.

On the kind of outside relationship:

   a. We can each have deeply personal and private friendships with
    persons of either sex.
   b. We can have sporadic sexual flings with others but no ongoing
    relationships.
   c. We can have ongoing sexual relationships but no one-night
    stands.
   d. We don't have to have the same style of outside sex.

On working out a mutually acceptable style:

   a. We do what the person who wants the greater freedom proposes.
   b. We do what the person who wants the more traditional relation-
    ship proposes.
   c. We negotiate some compromise.
   d. We try certain behaviors for a trial period.
   e. Both of us have veto power over what we don't like.
   f. Decisions like this are inevitably made by the person who has
    the most power in the relationship.

Postscript: The Other Person

This discussion has revolved around two people in a primary relationship.
However, by its nature, the supplemented style involves at least one more
person—the outside sexual partner. There is a real human being out there,
not just a picture in the centerfold of *Playboy* or *Playgirl*. What considerations apply to the other person?

If the encounter is to be casual, does the other partner clearly understand that? Do they agree willingly, or are they being manipulated? Do
they want a sex-only relationship, or are they planning, perhaps scheming,
for something more? If the relationship is to be more than casual, then is
it clear just what the limits are?

It would be convenient if a married person who seeks outside sex could
find another married or otherwise committed person "who seeks similar
for discreet matinees." They could set clearly defined limits to their relationship, fulfill their sexual desires, and return to their respective partners
more contented people. If their primary partners had agreed to the supplemented sexual style, "no one would be hurt." There are, however, many

combinations that are not so neatly defined—especially when a married person has an affair with an unmarried one.

The married person is often in the controlling position, since the married partner always has a primary relationship to fall back on. Unmarried participants may feel they have everything to lose if the affair ends and so accept it on terms dictated by their partners. Thus, they will cling to relationships that only partially fulfill their needs in the vain hope that more might be coming. The advice columns in your newspaper will confirm the number of single persons who get involved with married people and then start waiting for a promised divorce. Even when there is no promise, the single one may fabricate the hope. You have read stories like this: Jennifer got sexually involved with Roger about two years ago. At the time Roger told her he was comfortably married and had three lovely children, so divorce was out of the question. He wanted some exciting sex with little emotional involvement. At first Jennifer was content, but gradually she began to expect greater investment from Roger. After all, she had no other relationship from which to draw her emotional support. Roger went along with this until suddenly he realized he was putting his marriage in jeopardy. At this point he told Jennifer they would have to return to the old sex relationship or break off entirely. Jennifer was devastated by this ultimatum.

Being honest in such a situation takes talent. If you have been having outside sex, have you been able to be completely honest with your partner about what you expect from the relationship? Would you feel all right about the situation if you were in his or her place? Can you say that no one is being hurt?

Presumably people involved in a supplementary liaison are adults, and it would be demeaning for you to treat them as if they were children unable to take care of themselves. That fact, however, should not hide the possibility that people in sexual relationships are sometimes pitifully powerless to dictate the terms of their participation. If a supplementary relationship is to be considered successful, is it not reasonable to say that all the people involved should feel they are benefiting—or at least not being exploited—by the arrangement?

8

Forsaking All Others:
The Total Style

"I charge you both to remember that love and loyalty alone will avail as the foundation of a happy home. . . . No other human ties are more tender, no other vows more sacred than those you now assume." Charles and Irene are even more in love today than when they stood before the altar ten years ago and heard that charge. Their joy is to be together, preferably alone. They have a few friends, Charles has a job, and they belong to a church. But these are supports to their marriage, and none is allowed to compete with their own relationship. Neither of them has ever dreamed of intimacy with anyone else, much less anything sexual.

That is one image of what it is like to live with one person, forsaking all others, wrapping your whole life up in that relationship. There is, however, another image lurking in the shadows: Charles and Irene were married ten years ago in the aftermath of a whirlwind romance. Neither was surprised when they gradually settled into a routine existence. They have a few friends, Charles has a job, they belong to a church, but they don't put very much of themselves into any of these. Most evenings they are tired; they eat a quick and easy supper and then settle in front of the television. There is little conversation, only the occasional "Pass the peanuts, dear." Of course, neither of them has ever dreamed of having any outside sex. They have neither the energy nor the flair for such an adventure. If you were to ask one of them if they were happy, there would be a sigh and then, "I suppose so. Most people expect too much from life."

Is the total style the best of all possible worlds, or is it a sentimental image bound to tarnish like the silver frame on the wedding picture? In this chapter we will be looking at the advantages people seek and the problems they face in the pursuit of the total style. We must consider more than the sexual aspects of this style, however. When two people make their relationship central, working to satisfy most of each other's needs, then this becomes a style of life as well as a sexual style.

■ Imagine yourself in the following situations:

1. You have been offered a new position that would considerably increase your income and status. The job would entail working long hours and being away from home frequently. You and your partner have a very close relationship, which you both realize would suffer if you accepted this offer. Your partner has not said, "Don't take it," but clearly would prefer that you did not. What would you do? Rank the following three factors in your decision (put a 1 by the factor that would be most important in your decision, a 2 by what is next most important, and a 3 by what is least important):

_____ Your career

_____ Your partner's unspoken preference

_____ Maintaining your present close relationship

2. You are a pretty sexy person. You would like to have intercourse five or six times a week at least, but your partner is up for it only about once a week. You are thinking about "having it off" with a person at the office who obviously gets around. However, you realize that this might strain your otherwise lovely relationship. How would you resolve this dilemma? Rank the importance of each of these items in your consideration of the problem:

_____ Your personal satisfaction

_____ Your partner's desires

_____ Possible strain on your relationship

3. You're not very sexy. You are often tired after a long day. Once a week is plenty of sex for you. However, it seems as though your partner is ready to go every night. You like the companionship you two have together, but on the other hand you can't quite see how you can satisfy your partner's huge sexual appetite. How would you resolve this dilemma? Rank these items:

_____ Your personal desires

_____ Your partner's satisfaction

_____ The well-being of your relationship

4. You and your partner have a close, vital relationship. You have been asked to run a local charity. The organization accomplishes a

great deal, and you are flattered. However, it would consume masses of time and for months on end. Both you and your partner believe this will threaten the closeness you now have together. What would you do? Rank these items:

_____ The good you might do in this position

_____ Your sense of self-worth

_____ The well-being of your relationship

When you have considered all four situations, look over your rankings to see if any pattern emerges. You may have considered your own needs first, not necessarily out of selfishness but because you feel that to be your first responsibility. Or you may have considered your partner's needs and desires before anything else. Alternatively, you may naturally consider the well-being of your relationship before immediate gains for either you or your partner. You look for the solution that will be most likely to keep the relationship happy and growing: "If things are going well between us, then they go well for each of us." Can you see in your rankings a tendency either to give more weight to individual needs or to put relational needs before anything else?

People who like the total style make their relationship the top priority in their lives. They do not stress their own needs, or even the individual needs of a partner, so much as the quality of their relationship. That person who was asked to run a charity might benefit personally, and for that matter the partner might also benefit, but their attention to each other will be diluted, they feel, and their relationship will no longer be primary. Not everyone will expect it to turn out this way, of course. A person living a supplemented style may say, "We each have to have our own thing going before we can be good partners." But people who strive for a total style see their own needs as best fulfilled in an intense and rather exclusive intimacy.

Probably most of us share the deep yearning for intimacy that the total style prizes so highly. Aficionados of totalism point to the possibility of overcoming loneliness and alienation in a deep mingling of body, mind, and soul. The complexities of modern life have fragmented relationships and battered the individual. In the strength of a profound intimacy some of this fragmentation is overcome. You can be a person and not just fifteen different computer numbers.

Is this total style a realistic goal? Is there anyone in the world you would want to be with all the time? Do you want a total relationship?

Suppose you inherited $2 million, after taxes. You no longer have to work. You have all the time in the world to spend with your partner if you should wish to do so. What would you do? Would you spend all or most of your time alone with your partner, or would you need other people around you? Are there any other people in particular with whom you would wish to spend your time? What activities would you do alone and what with your partner? How large a part would sex play in your relationship? Would you be sexually exclusive?

How difficult is it for you to imagine nearly constant togetherness? Does it seem boring? Confining? Lonely? Do you want more freedom and privacy? Or does the sense of closeness, sharing, and intimacy that could arise in such a situation appeal to you? Does your present occupation protect you from too much closeness, or does it prevent you from having as much as you want?

"To be intimate" is sometimes taken to mean having sexual intercourse. This euphemism, common in courts of law, implies that you can be intimate for a few minutes and virtually unknown to each other before and after. "Were you intimate with _____ on the afternoon of _____, and again on the morning of _____?" asks the prosecuting attorney. Persons pursuing the total style would never understand intimacy in that narrow sense. Their reflections might go something like this: "Intimacy is more than sex. Sometimes sex is about as intimate as buying a loaf of bread at the supermarket. Real intimacy involves sharing joy and pain, anger and love, work and play, body and mind. Sharing on these levels means sharing each other's whole being. Of course, there is no such thing as complete sharing or total union. Yet it is only by striving for this ideal that two people engage each other deeply enough to feel the warmth, closeness, happiness, and sense of oneness that intimacy can bring. If two people go elsewhere to seek satisfaction, how can they expect to grow in intimacy? Escaping from problems in a relationship never resolves them, but working them through can bring two people much closer together."

How do you react to this? Is struggle necessary for the development of intimacy? Or does it just happen, just the way sexual intimacy does? How does sexual involvement affect intimacy for you? Do they always go together? Can they be separated?

If you have been in an important relationship with another person for quite a while, have you ever experienced anything like the "seven-year itch" or a desire to take a break from the arrangement? Have you ever wanted to have an affair, go off on your own, do something wild? If so, how did you cope with the itch? If you have never been in this situation, imagine yourself in this position now. What would you do?

1. Go off and not come back.
2. Go off and then come back to the old pattern.
3. Take up a supplemented sexual style from now on.
4. Remain at home, wishing you had done something different.
5. Talk yourself out of these feelings.
6. Talk your feelings over with your partner.
7. _____

Did, or would, your course of action lead to greater or less intimacy with your partner? What does this say about your view of intimacy and the total style?

Strangely, most of us both desire intimacy and fear it. Thus, a great relationship can offer the promise of the fulfillment of all our yearnings for closeness, or it can be a threat, seeming to submerge us in a sea of togetherness. Some may stress the threat. The person in the total style stresses the promise. In intimacy the self is realized, not negated.

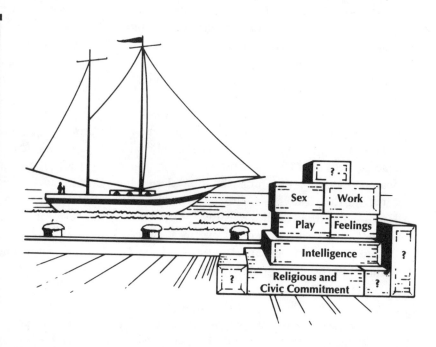

Picture for a moment your primary relationship. What are its treasures, the previous cargoes of your life? Do you want to entrust all of these treasures to this one vessel, your primary relationship? Or might that sink it? Mark what proportion of each cargo you would like to put in that ship. Where would you like to put the rest of the cargo: in other sexual relationships, in friendships, or on yourself?

Essential to the achievement of intimacy in more than one or two of these areas is a desire to spend large amounts of time together. Closeness and intimacy are not usually developed by grabbing a stand-up bite at the snack bar four nights a week, running off in different directions, returning hours later, staving off sleep only long enough to mumble, "G'night." Neither is intimacy likely to result from a side-by-side existence in front of the television screen. Quality, as well as quantity, of time spent together is important. True, some people can manage an intimate relationship on much less time spent together than others. They interact quickly, frequently, meaningfully, in the time they have together. Yet there seems to be a certain minimum amount of time, more or less for different people, that must be devoted to mutual sharing if a relationship of quality is to flourish.

Some people exercise astonishing ingenuity in keeping distance between themselves and their partners. Karen and Ben are both professionals. Karen's job requires that she frequently attend evening meetings. Ben is usually at home evenings, but he often brings home a briefcase full of papers to look over. If Karen is not home for dinner, Ben grabs a bite, fixes a drink, and sits reading a magazine "to relax a bit" before he gets to work. About ten o'clock Karen returns, saying she is ready "to play." Ben, however, replies that he has to work—he has brought home this big briefcase of . . . Karen amuses herself while Ben sets about his papers. In an hour or two he seeks out Karen, but by then she has fallen asleep or is too engrossed in a new novel to be bothered.

Can you see any similar pattern in your own life? Could you and your partner arrange schedules so that you could spend more time together? Would you want to do this?

How do you spend your free time right now? Make a list of twenty things you like to do. Gather your courage and code your list:

A is for things you do *alone*.

O is for things you do with *others*, not including your partner.

P is for things you do with your *partner*.

(You may have more than one letter by some activities. For example, you may sometimes go skiing with your partner and sometimes alone.)

> Do you and your partner share many activities together? Are there things you wish your partner would do with you that he or she currently doesn't? Are there things you enjoy doing that your partner disapproves of?
>
> W is for things you *want* to do with your partner but don't.
>
> D is for things you like to do of which your partner *disapproves*.

If many of your activities have only an A by them, you may value your privacy highly. If many have an O by them but no P, and you like it that way, you are supplementing your primary relationship. If many of your activities have a P by them, you may have a total relationship—at least, if you like it that way. However, many of your activities may have an A and/or O by them, followed by a W or D. Have any of these activities created conflicts in your relationship? If you have put a W by several activities, perhaps you wish to have a more total relationship than your partner does. Have you ever discussed more participation in activities with your partner? But think twice before you ask your partner, a seeded tennis player, to play with you, a beginner.

This list can be useful to do with a partner. List and code your activities independently. Try to guess which activities are on your partner's list, which your partner would like to share with you, and which your partner thinks you disapprove of. Have him or her make the same guesses about your list. Do you find any surprises? We frequently find that partners imagine each other disapproving more than is actually true. Often, too, one partner is not aware that the other wishes they could both participate in some particular activity: "Oh, really, I never dreamed you would want to go parachute jumping with me!"

You, You, You . . . Never Anyone but You

It will come as no surprise that people who pursue the total style almost always choose to be sexually exclusive. If they compromise anything in trying to be total, it is not sex. Actually, sex is the one thing that is easiest to keep total, at least in behavior. One's eyes or imagination may wander unbidden, but one's hands or genitals are under considerable control. By contrast, social and emotional enjoyments cannot be kept so rigidly within a relationship. We go to work, meet people, read books, attend the ballet or the theater. Presumably we derive satisfaction from these encounters. Therefore, the most total of relationships is not the only source of all satisfaction. But sex is different. It is possible for you to get all of your sexual enjoyment from your own partner—almost, anyway.

To persons who value the total style, outside sex is an obvious drain on energy that would otherwise be devoted to their primary relationship. This energy loss is not just sexual energy. Sex will usually be understood by a person in a total style as appropriate only when there is some depth of relationship. Therefore, to engage in outside sex is to have an important emotional investment in the supplementary person and to lessen the importance of the primary relationship. "We have a great thing going with each other. You never know what you might lose fooling around with somebody else." Stability and security are important for the development of a good relationship. If you have it, why risk it?

For such people sexual exclusivity is not a burden but a privilege. They might be nonexpressive—or they may have chosen a highly expressive sexual style, enjoying lots of "sexual fun." Some of the joy comes from having a sexual partner whose sexual moods and modes are thoroughly familiar, with whom one is quite secure and at ease. The security of the good relationship opens the door to experimentation, to the development of practiced sensitivity. No sometime bed partner can ever provide that. Knowing what the partner likes, being able to fulfill that desire—and being fulfilled in return—those are the special rewards of an exclusive style.

There may be a few people who seek a total style and are not sexually exclusive. These would be people who do not feel that sex is very important to them or to their relationship. It therefore makes little difference one way or the other to the achievement of intimacy. If sex is not an important part of how they relate, then it is not important whether either relates sexually to other people.

For others it is precisely the rejection of sexual exclusivity that leads them to reject the total style. "I can't imagine myself having intercourse with only one person for the rest of my life, much less limiting my close and intimate relationships to that one person." Many people today, and especially women, feel that sex is the key that can unlock the gates to wider and fuller relationships, that we must throw over the tired, old morality that artificially contorts the natural shape of human emotions. Others, however, feel sexual freedom unlocks sluice gates, releasing a flood of muddied relationships.

Making and Keeping Promises

Giving a partnership high, or even top, priority in one's life, working through differences to deeper levels of intimacy, spending large amounts of time together, being sexually exclusive—that indeed requires a high degree of commitment from two people. For most this commitment seems best secured in marriage. This legally and often religiously binding arrangement offers some expectation that spouses will not split the moment that they have an argument about who does the dishes. Behind this is a realism that anticipates pain and even tragedy in human affairs. The vows are a symbol of a willingness and an intention not only to enjoy life together but to persevere together when the going gets rough.

Some would argue, perhaps including you, that marriage is a license for most partners to relax and to stop trying to enrich their relationship. Beer bellies and bulging hips are one measure of the care partners stop taking to be attractive to each other. It is ridiculous to think that making a few promises will do any good. The vows may actually lessen people's commitment to maintaining the quality of a relationship day in and day out. The only real commitment is that which is renewed daily. That is certainly not ensured by legal or religious sanctions. If you don't lean on such crutches, you will work harder to provide an environment in which to struggle and grow together. Without one of those "till death do us part" contracts, you will at every moment know you are staying together because you want to and not because some bit of paper says you must. Why not find a style of living with your partner that promises what a vow cannot: constant commitment, signified by your continued investment in each other?

What *degree* of commitment do you want in a relationship? Place yourself on this line:

None	Moderate	High

What *kind* of commitment do you want in a relationship?

None directly expressed	Informal, nonlegal	Everything signed, sealed, and delivered

As you thought about these options, did you experience any anxiety? On the one side, anxiety may arise at the thought of not knowing what the expectations are, or whether indeed there are any: "Can I count on my partner? What weird direction might things take?" The uncertainty is unsettling. On the other side, anxiety may come from a fear of entrapment: "All those expectations and promises . . . always trying to meet demands handed down to us. . . . How can I promise to feel the way I do now twenty years from now?" Commitments, too heavy and too detailed, may box us in, restricting our freedom to become what we really are.

The appeal of the total style is greatest for those who prefer to have expectations defined. To others, this is the style most susceptible to feelings of restriction. If the only way to have your needs satisfied is from your partner, you are apt to forgo getting certain needs met. Resentment feeds on empty spaces filled only with yearning for what is not there.

An even more common criticism of totalism is the danger of boredom. Everything is arranged in advance: no surprises, just move from initial intimacy to ever deeper intimacy. How can the fresh and the creative enter this tight little circle of two? Routines develop over time, hardening into thinking automation. Sex becomes dull, predictable—"every third night at 10 P.M." Of course, the total relationship doesn't have to turn out this way, but the question is, Will it for you? If you choose this style, what will you do to prevent it from becoming a feather comforter filled with five-pound weights?

Still another set of reservations about the total style arises from the belief that unrealistic expectations can result. Too much idealism, romantic sentimentality, promises from here to eternity, and such high standards of commitment and great expectations of intimate intensity that no human being can possibly measure up—these can lead to conflict, loss of the sense of self-worth, or a retreat from trying to be total.

Finally, you may hear the argument that the total style is basically selfish. The supplemented style may present the danger of individual selfishness, but the total style is subject to "relational selfishness." Two people may be so protective of their relationship that they are quite willing to hurt others or ignore the rest of the world to enhance their own bond. People living the total style may be aware of this accusation. In Cuber and Haroff's interviews with the "significant Americans," some of the people pursuing a total relationship said they tried to hide from others the fact that they wanted to be together so much. They were aware that other people thought their closeness to be "unnatural" or "peculiar."[1] They chose this style in spite of their critics, believing the benefits outweighed that disadvantage.

So, what do you think? Is the total style a will-o'-the-wisp, forever just beyond the reach of aspiring lovers? Or is it the only way for love really to be love? Clearly, many more people dream about being in a total relationship than ever come close to having one. Why is that? Is it because it is an impossible dream? Or is it because people would rather talk than act and thus do not make the simple commitments necessary to achieve a really loving relationship?

9

Kids: The Procreative Style

Okay—so you've found the partner of your dreams, you've gotten married, you've even made the down payment on a place of your own. There is just one thing missing: the pitter-patter of little feet. There are no little Bobbys and Suzies toddling about the nursery, no little bundles of joy for grandparents to beam at and brag about.

Are you ready to throw this book at us? Are you groaning, "Oh, no! Not another person telling us we should have kids"? Until recently children have been the almost inevitable result of sexual intercourse. Moreover, it was necessary to have many children for families, tribes, nations, or indeed the human race, to survive. The societal message was that you should have children—within wedlock, of course.

Today the self-interest of an individual family, tribe, or nation may still at times be on the side of a high birthrate. But there is little doubt that the welfare of the human race as a whole is on the side of a drastically lower birthrate. Lower infant mortality, longer life expectancy, and the gradual depletion of natural resources are among the many factors that have combined to make a world population problem. But many people now consider babies less desirable. Furthermore, babies no longer need to be the inevitable result of sexual intercourse. The technology for preventing childbirth and the development of a world population problem together are rapidly and dramatically changing attitudes toward having children. For the first time in human history many people are considering . . .

Whether . . . How Many . . . When?

Imagine yourself as very old and coming to the end of your life. Let the years between now and then be whatever you want them to be. Look back over your life. Now write an obituary for yourself, listing those things for which you want most to be remembered.

How traditional is your obituary? Does it include the usual line: "He/she is survived by a wife/husband and X children and Y grandchildren"? If so, is it there because you genuinely want children to be an important part of your life, or because it is expected that you will have children, and so include them in your obituary? We are generally taught not only that we ought to have children but also that we *ought to want to have* children. This is not as unreasonable as it sounds, since it would be unfortunate to have unwanted children out of duty. Nevertheless, "to want what we ought to want" can be something of an emotional contortion. Do you genuinely want it, or do you want it only because you ought to?

Roz and Tim had been married about ten years and were in their early thirties when they finally decided to have a child. For a long time they did not think they wanted to have children. But, as they saw their middle years approaching, they realized that it was now or never and that they were afraid they might miss out on real happiness if they passed up having their own family. Roz decided she would take her chances with removing herself from the job market for a couple of years. She did not want to have a child and then immediately hand the baby over to someone else to raise. Tim withdrew from a number of community activities so as to be at home more and to give Roz an opportunity to keep up a few of her outside interests. To their delight, they found it much easier than they had expected to make these life-style adjustments. The rewards of watching their baby grow, of feeling somehow fulfilled in their own sexuality by the birth, of sensing the continuity of family line, all combined to enrich and reward their own relationship.

Charles and Phyllis were also a reasonably contented childless couple, but they both had parents who regularly pressured them to have children. Sometimes this was done very directly: "Don't you think it's time you two started a family?" Other times the pressure was more subtle. One day Phyllis stumbled across a box in her parents' attic labeled, "Toys for our grandchildren—Alas, hope fades!" Eventually Charles and Phyllis began saying to each other, "Well, perhaps we should have a child. It would make our parents so happy." Then, when their best friends, another previously childless couple, announced that they were about to become parents, the matter was settled. Charles and Phyllis decided to have a child. When the birth approached, Charles insisted that Phyllis quit her job, since he earned enough to support them amply. However, he did not curtail any of his own activities. Thus, after the initial excitement of the birth wore off, Phyllis found herself sitting at home alone most of the time with a tiny human who could only eat, sleep, wet, and cry. Soon she was crying a lot, too. She began resenting Charles bitterly for having thought a child would be such a good idea and for forcing her to stop work. Charles, in turn, started grumbling that it hadn't been his idea to have a child, and why was it that Phyllis wasn't any fun to be around anymore?

It has been the traditional procreative view that "to be vital and growing, a marital pair needs mutual investment in children."[1] Children enrich a couple's lives and help to give them a sense of continuity in a world of flux and change. They deepen the couple's commitment, or investment, in each other, which in turn gives more stability to the family. The more stable a family is, the happier it is likely to be. Moreover, a stable family contributes to the maintenance of a stable society.

Recently, however, research has appeared that challenges the notion that children bring stability and happiness to couples. Sociologist Jessie Bernard has marshaled evidence that childless marriages may be happier ones. Another study, of the subjective feelings about life satisfaction, has shown that the happiness of young married persons falls suddenly and significantly with the birth of children, not to rise again until the children are grown and about to leave home. Couples with children apparently experience more stress and pressure than any other group, and the mothers feel this more acutely than the fathers.[2]

Obviously, you should not take this research to mean that you personally should give up the notion of having children. You may or may not be among the percentage who find themselves less happy with children. There are couples like Roz and Tim who find joy and enrichment in having children, just as there are couples like Charles and Phyllis who find children disruptive to their life satisfactions. Only you can know which couple you are like.

Construct a "life-world" in your imagination. Draw a circle representing your life, your resources (time, energy, money, emotional commitment, and so on). Shade a portion of this circle to represent how much of yourself, your resources, you would like to have invested in children (as opposed to job, spouse, other relatives, friends, hobbies, and so on). Do you want this shaded portion to be large or small? Do you want to place it in the center, around the edge, or in a section of the circle? Ponder this for a while. Then shade quite darkly the part of this lightly shaded portion that represents your willingness to "sacrifice" for the sake of your children. Is this part large or small? Is it necessary to have such a section at all? Is all this fun to think about, or is it threatening and anxiety producing?

If you are unclear whether you want children because you really want them or only because you ought to want them, you will find it useful to seek out opportunities to be with children. You might try to experience children of various ages in a variety of situations. You might talk to some couples who are already parents. No matter how these experiences may influence you, there is no doubt that you will make more satisfying decisions if you are aware of your own feelings, your anxieties as well as your hopes.

Rational and practical questions need to be faced, too, but to answer rational questions rationally requires that you be clear about what your emotions are. Then you can with greater confidence consider practical questions such as financial resources, adequacy of housing, educational opportunities, and quality of life available in the community. Of course, none of these matters can be answered by you alone, unless perhaps you are a single woman considering having a child of your own. Otherwise, you and your partner need to reflect together on your attitudes and feelings, as well as on the rational questions, in order to come to a common answer.

If you decide for children, you still face the other two questions: How many? And when? You could choose to have as many children as might result from your acts of intercourse—let nature take its course. Chances are overwhelming, however, that you do not want to be like the Old Woman Who Lived in a Shoe. You will decide to limit childbirth at least to some degree. Perhaps you wish first to finish your education, get established in your profession, buy a house, wait until another child is older, or recover from a serious illness or operation. Whatever your reasons, you will be asking, "How are we going to limit or space births?" The choices spread out like this:

Abstinence	Contraception	Abortion	Sterilization
Celibacy	Pill	Morning-after pill	Tubal ligation
Rhythm method	IUD	Abortion:	Vasectomy
	Condom	first trimester	
	Diaphragm	second trimester	
	Spermatocidal		
	foams and		
	jellies		

Here are five questions you may wish to ask about any method of contraception you are considering:

1. How effective is the method in controlling or preventing conception? The various alternatives have been tested for degree of effectiveness. With present technology the rhythm method is the least effective, then comes the condom, the diaphragm, the intrauterine device (IUD), and the pill. Sterilization is the most effective method. The technology may change tomorrow, and you will want to keep abreast of it.

2. What, if any, are the comparative health risks to me or my partner of this method? At present all legal forms of contraception, sterilization, and abortion when properly carried out are safer for the physical health of the woman, on a statistical basis, than is childbirth itself. There is an emerging documentation of health risks from the pill and the IUD. There is no known health risk from the condom or diaphragm and only the minute risks of ordinary minor surgical procedures in the case of vasectomy.

3. What is the degree of certainty that I (we) will use this method correctly and in time? Abstinence is quite certain if it is always followed, but that is not necessarily easy. There is many a slip between the cup and the lip. Sterilization is quite certain, but not presently reversible.

4. What, if any, are my (our) tastes or preferences in relation to these methods? Creams, foams, plastics, pills—any one of these may be a pleasant addition or a distasteful duty to you personally. For one couple the placing of a condom on the penis is an enjoyable part of their love play. For another using a condom is like going swimming in a raincoat.

5. What role do other principles play in my (our) choice of method? Values derived from religious or moral ideas influence each of the earlier questions. You may be committed to specific rules that prohibit one or another of these procedures. For example, you may consider abortion to

be the taking of human life and therefore wrong regardless of any other consideration.[3]

What is your decision about children? This year? Next year? Sometime? Never?

Turned-on Parents?

At some point in almost every workshop we conduct on sexual values, someone will say, "You know, I can never quite imagine that my mother and father actually have sex." This remark always produces a chorus of knowing agreement. Parents hide their sexuality from their children, and the children tend to think of their parents as sexless. It requires a feat of colorful imagination to think that they actually had sexual intercourse, even in order for one's own birth to have taken place. To further believe that one's parents have sex for the pleasure of it staggers the imagination. As one young man put it, "Well, I guess I can go along with the idea that my parents had sex once or twice."

How easy is it for you to imagine? Is this just a sexual hang-up of most adults? Or is it part and parcel of the procreative view of sex? Let's sort out some of the issues.

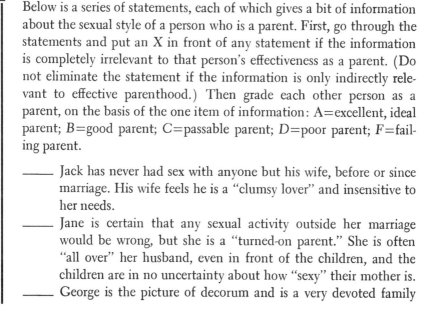

Below is a series of statements, each of which gives a bit of information about the sexual style of a person who is a parent. First, go through the statements and put an X in front of any statement if the information is completely irrelevant to that person's effectiveness as a parent. (Do not eliminate the statement if the information is only indirectly relevant to effective parenthood.) Then grade each other person as a parent, on the basis of the one item of information: A=excellent, ideal parent; B=good parent; C=passable parent; D=poor parent; F=failing parent.

_____ Jack has never had sex with anyone but his wife, before or since marriage. His wife feels he is a "clumsy lover" and insensitive to her needs.
_____ Jane is certain that any sexual activity outside her marriage would be wrong, but she is a "turned-on parent." She is often "all over" her husband, even in front of the children, and the children are in no uncertainty about how "sexy" their mother is.
_____ George is the picture of decorum and is a very devoted family

man. Actually he has frequent outside sexual relationships, but these are done so discreetly that no one ever suspects.

_____ Karen believes in being completely open with her children about sex. She and her husband arrange to have intercourse in relative privacy but do not hide what they are doing and are quite matter-of-fact about it if the children happen in, as has occurred on occasions.

_____ Charles is strictly monogamous but has more frequent sexual needs than his wife. With her consent, he deals with this by frequent masturbation.

_____ Marlene feels free to have sex with whomever she wishes. She believes it would be dishonest to hide this from the children. She sometimes has a lover come to the house, and if the children are there, she simply tells them that she and her friend want to go to bed together and want to be left undisturbed.

_____ Hal is what his wife calls "an oversexed, wonderful lover." He is always ready to jump into bed with her, often trying "something new and different." He rejects all sexual contact with anyone else, and he is very careful never to display or discuss his sexual attitudes in front of their small children.

_____ Jeanne has remained faithful and monogamous to her husband, but she suspects that he has had affairs. She is resentful because she keeps passing up sexual opportunities she would have liked to pursue with other men.

_____ John and his wife have agreed to have sex with other people, but they do so without reporting to each other. John does not believe in having their children know about this arrangement, since he feels it would upset them.

_____ Mary does not believe her sexual "affairs" in any way affect her love for her husband or her children. She has her husband's agreement, but she is very careful that no one knows about her outside sex, since she does not want it to embarrass her family.

_____ Joyce's husband left her and the children three years ago, and since then she has formed a primary relationship with another woman. Although they do not relate sexually in front of the children, Joyce has told them about the relationship and the need to keep quiet about it outside the family.

As you study the statements in this exercise, you will find three major questions emerging: (1) How much should children know about their parents' sexuality? (2) Is it necessary to be sexually exclusive in order to be an effective parent? (3) How sexy can one be and still be an effective parent?

Openness or secrecy with children about parental sexuality involves some issues about which there is relevant technical information. Parents who are hysterically fearful of their children's learning anything about their sexuality communicate anxious attitudes to their children. On the other hand, children who actually see adults in coitus, and especially their parents, can be traumatized by that experience. Fortunately, the choices most parents make will be between these two extremes.

Assume that your partner has just come in and starts giving you a very passionate embrace. Your children are watching television in the adjoining room. Do you gently push him or her away and say, "Not now, darling. What would the children think?" Or do you join in the embrace wholeheartedly? Are you embarrassed if the children see any hint of sexuality in your behavior? Where do you draw the line in your sexual behavior if the children are apt to see you: at a warm kiss, a passionate embrace, breast or genital stimulation with your clothes on? How far would you go? Would the age of your children make any difference?

Now suppose that you do not expect your children to appear. You are making love at night, behind closed doors. Suddenly your five-year-old pushes open the door, asking for solace after a bad dream. How would you feel? What would you do? What would you say? Would you like to be matter-of-fact about this? What are the chances that you could manage not to communicate hysteria? Would your reactions be the same if it were your thirteen-year-old who thoughtlessly barged into your bedroom to tell you who won the basketball game? How would you handle the situation then?

There are obvious problems with pretending that parental sex does not exist. It conflicts with the facts! It contributes to the mysterious and even threatening specter that sex may present to the developing child. Nevertheless, it does little good to affect a "cool" you do not possess. A useful way to handle this, especially with an older child, is to talk about your discomfort and to move from that to your belief that both what happened and your discomfort are okay. With a younger child, it is very important to remain with the child and encourage the expression of feelings of confusion, helping him or her to realize that everything is all right. Small children sometimes misunderstand coitus as a fight, and parental fright may support that illusion.

There is disagreement about the effect family nudity has on the sexual development of the child. Some psychologists believe that nudity in the family, provided it is not imposed on children who have already developed a personal modesty, contributes to a healthy appreciation and acceptance of the body and sex. Others believe that family nudity may stimulate sexual or incestuous feelings that the child has no way of handling. Still others say that family nudity desensitizes older children to erotic stimulation and reduces normal sexual interest. Subsequent studies may shed further light on this, but for now the decisive issues are the values of the parents and the behavior with which they and their children are most comfortable. Running around without your clothes on, trying to be "liberated" while you nervously perspire and blush, is apt to be as unsettling for children as were you to run shrieking for a towel if they should inadvertently see you nude.

Openness with children takes on another facet when parents engage in sexual styles that do not fit the usual public pattern of monogamous marriage. If you have chosen a supplemented style and are a parent, for example, you have some important decisions to make. You can choose to keep your sexual values completely secret from your children. You can choose to be completely open, allowing them to meet and get to know your other sexual partners. Or you can keep the details of your relationships private, while you gradually allow your children to know the values on which you base your sexual existence.

These decisions depend not only on how comfortable you are with the choices you make; they also depend upon how comfortable your children turn out to be with the information as you communicate it. We know of only a very few couples who are able to be open with teenaged children about the fact that they engage in extramarital sex. And there is a marked tendency for the children to reject the behavior. It is our unproved hypothesis that teenagers largely accept premarital intercourse, but in the romanticism of this stage, they believe that they themselves will be monogamous once they meet the right person and are married. They are hostile toward behavior in their parents that they reject for themselves. This may change if the whole social climate becomes more permissive, but for now there are large areas of conflict even in those who have been raised in the most permissive atmospheres.

These considerations mean that some people pursue nonexclusive sexual styles until they have children and then switch to exclusive monogamy. Others believe that it is as important to their children as to themselves that they live out a sexual style that has meaning and integrity for them. Attitudes toward sexual openness, then, may influence how a person answers the question of whether it is necessary to be sexually exclusive in order to be an effective parent.

Traditionally, parenthood and a supplemented sexual style have been considered incompatible. If an affair happened, that was too bad. Worse, however, was that it should be known. The affair in itself threatened family stability. Knowledge of it could prove even more destructive. Do you feel this still holds true? Has contraception made this style more reasonable for parents to pursue? Or do you believe that the stability of the family is still usually threatened by the outside sexual activity of parents? Is there one style of sexual behavior appropriate to childless couples and another to those with children?

Probably, however, it is the third question that interests most people: How sexy or sexually expressive can one be and still be an effective parent? The cultural messages about this are not very direct. Your mother probably did not tell you, "Don't have fun in bed because you will be a poor parent!" However, you may have heard, "Oh, not now, George! I have to iron the clothes" (or do the dishes, mend Johnny's socks, . . .). Or, "For goodness' sake, Hazel, take that dress off. You look like a tart in that outfit." Or, "George, really! Why don't you act your age?" The unspoken assumption is that a woman should be sexy to catch her man but that once she has done this, she should start dressing and acting in a manner more befitting a wife and mother. The man, in his turn, is expected to get his sexual drive toned down by the time the first child is born so that he is not tempted to go philandering. The assumption is that his wife will become less attractive to him with childbearing and age.

If moving to a less sexually expressive style is a reasoned and comfortable choice, then well and good. If it is forced on marital partners like an old-fashioned nightgown, then it is absurd. If you would like to leave the ironing and hop into bed for an hour, is there something wrong with that? Can you not expect, demand, and arrange "privacy time" for yourselves? Do you have to be on twenty-four-hour call to your children? If you are parents wondering what place sex now has for you, we suggest that you each make a list of priorities in your life. Where does sex come in each list? What would you have to do to adjust your priorities comfortably to one another?

Sex cannot be measured in the amount of time it requires, by comparison to a job or housework. It does not take long hours to have intercourse. But it does require a setting in which energy is available for erotic enjoyment. This is why it is important to decide how high a priority you put on sex. We talk with devoted couples who don't know what to do in order to get the excitement back into sex but who continue to have sex at the end of exhausting days. When they decide to move sex up in importance, this too easily means having sex more often. Then it becomes simply a greater energy drain and even less enjoyable. To develop a more erotic style requires changing priorities so that sex is in a relaxed and leisurely setting at a time when your energy and privacy are available. Sex isn't sexy when a responsibility is so pressing that it seems to stand by the bed like a disapproving observer.

It can be very uncomfortable to realize that sex is in competition with a job interview, a church committee, or the PTA. It is, however, a fact. We throw gobs of energy down the drain by longing for the impossible. It is not possible for most of us, ordinary mortals as we are, to be brilliant in our jobs, constantly attentive parents, terribly responsible in the community, marvelous housekeepers or gardeners, snappy dressers, and great in bed. How about choosing where the energy will go and then accepting the limitations those choices involve? After all, it is not at all clear that you would be happier if you did accomplish all those grand things! The next time you see someone who appears to do so, give yourself the luxury of some "sour grapes": "Well, if they're so good at all that, they must be lousy in bed."

10

Choosing a Way to Choose

We have now completed our tour of sexual styles. As we have moved among the various styles, you have been making choices, accepting or rejecting a little from this one, a lot from that one. Some of these choices were very easy, made quickly and almost without thought. Others, however, were difficult. You may even have considered giving up the journey. But no, you persisted with courage and strength in search of your own sexual values.

This does not mean, of course, that you have resolved all sexual issues in your life. That would be expecting something superhuman of yourself. More likely, in sorting out your sexual values, you may even have discovered new dilemmas, new choices or options. You may, for example, now be considering trying a new sexual style. In any case, important decisions remain to be made.

Perhaps the most important choice you make is the choice of a way of choosing. How do you go about making decisions? Do you let happen whatever will? Do you act on intuition, impulse, or that "certain feeling"? Do you carefully calculate the consequences of each possible course of action? Do you seek advice from someone more knowledgeable than you? At this point you can take stock of how far you have come in choosing your sexual style by considering the five ways that people usually make sexual choices. Which ways do you use most?

Sexual Destiny: "Whatever Will Be, Will Be"

How much freedom do you actually have to choose your sexual style? Do you ever look at people living different sexual styles and say to yourself, "That style seems great, but it can never be mine. You can't make crepes suzette out of mashed potatoes." Some people say this all the time and keep change from happening by acting as if everything is destined to be as it is. At the other extreme are those ambitious souls who constantly try to reshape themselves and the world.

People who discuss their sexual confusions with us usually don't believe they can reshape the world, but they do assume they have some control over their own behavior. (We do too, or we wouldn't have bothered writing this book.) The question is, How much and what kind of control? This is a highly personal judgment that affects our actions constantly.

It is important to be realistic about the limitations on our freedom. Expecting the impossible from ourselves can be as disappointing as awaiting miracles from others. Our biology, for example, provides a remarkable range of possibilities but also, in the end, limits us. No amount of trying is likely to give a man twenty-five orgasms a day. Male physiology sees to that. Likewise, positions in lovemaking are finally restricted by the physical contortions of which the human body is capable. No amount of imagination can change that.

Another limitation on sexual choice is our situation in life. Housing arrangements, family responsibilities, and job expectations are among the many factors that may restrict the sexual styles you can consider. The most important limitation of all may be a lover or spouse. Some of these restrictions are imposed by fact or grim necessity, but others by lack of imagination, by illusions, or by deliberate restriction of choice. We frequently hear people say, "I'd like to have more time and energy for sex, but I simply can't afford to work any less than I do." The people who say this may be making $8,000 or $50,000 a year. They say they have no choice, but what many really mean is that the price for changing their sexual style is too high. That is fine, as long as they are aware that they have made a choice and are not frustrated by the illusion that they are helpless victims.

Here is a list of outside influences that may put limits on your sexual style:

Job/career	Unavailability of partners
Other interests/activities	Feelings of inadequacy
Living arrangements	Other fears/anxieties
Partner's needs	Expectations of friends
Health	Legal restrictions
Obligations to children	Finances
Obligations to other family members	Moral/religious beliefs
Community/social responsibilities	Others _____ _____

Cross out those that you feel do not limit your sexual style to any significant degree. Underline those over which, practically speaking, you have no real control. Finally, place an asterisk before the two or three items that place the most important limitations on you.

Now ponder the items in the list that you feel are beyond your control. Some of them surely are. But are there some factors that you have underlined that are really changeable if you wanted to change them badly enough?

Another important issue is how much you choose by letting events take their course. "The moment our eyes met I knew we were destined to be lovers. I could no more resist the attraction than order a twenty-five-hour day." This may sound like soap opera to you, or it may sound like a realism that recognizes that events run their course regardless of human will. People often feel a casual sexual encounter to be all right if it seems natural or irresistible. They will not actively seek a casual encounter, but neither will they refuse an attractive sexual invitation if one should present itself. What about you? How much responsibility do you want to take for maintaining a total style or seeking a casual one? How much responsibility do you wish to take for having children?

One of the unsatisfying ways of trying to get out of responsibility for our choices is to believe that we have no choice when in fact we do. It is true that values and attitudes absorbed from birth onward are not easily dissolved. They produce ideas and expectations that are a part of the very fiber of our thinking and feeling. It is unwise to ignore them. But this does not mean that you need be completely imprisoned by your origins, by values you did not choose for yourself. The very fact that so many of us are changing so fast in our attitudes and behavior provides both the opportunity and the necessity for clarifying our value choices. Knowing the difference between things you can change and those you cannot can contribute significantly to the satisfaction you feel in the choices you make.

Sexual Tastes: "I Like It, I Like It"

No matter what sexual style you choose, taste is bound to enter into your decision to some degree: your taste or society's taste. In fact, there is a point of view that regards all sexual issues as matters of taste. When a person says, "Adultery is wrong," what is really meant is, "I don't like adultery." Making moral statements about sex is an attempt to give authority to what are really personal desires. What each person prefers is all that should matter.

Most people, however, do not take such an extreme stand. Some believe that although sex itself is not a moral issue, a sexual act may be wrong because of other, nonsexual factors. Intercourse is not wrong, but rape is because of the force and violence used. As long as selfishness or some other harmful nonsexual factor does not intervene, then sex is simply a matter of taste or preference. We simply have to mesh our preferences with those of others who have similar tastes.

Others say that sex is a mixture of moral and aesthetic issues. Some acts involve no principles or consequences beyond the desire: "I prefer intercourse in the morning." But other acts involve long-range consequences: intercourse without contraception includes the possibility of pregnancy. Or they involve a principle: "I vowed never to have intercourse outside marriage." If you act contrary to your own taste, you will be disappointed and have an unpleasant time. If you act contrary to your own moral judgment, then you will feel remorse or guilt—even if you enjoyed the experience at the time.

An increasing number of people, including many sexologists, believe that our sexual hang-ups are often the result of moralizing about behavior better understood as a matter of taste. If we apply moral judgment to all our sexual behavior, then we are likely to feel guilty about our preferences and to reject our own sexual feelings.

Are you aware of when you are making moral judgments and when you are simply expressing preferences? What mix of aesthetic and moral judgment guides your sexual behavior? Anxiety and uncertainty are often the result of confusing your moral and aesthetic choices. If you clarify your thinking on what this difference is for you, you may experience fewer mornings of remorse. Remember, a sexual behavior is an aesthetic issue for you if you engage in it or shun it primarily as a matter of taste or preference. Nothing else influences your choice significantly. A sexual behavior is a moral issue for you if some other principle is the major influence in your choice. This other principle might be an evaluation of consequences, a principle such as the Golden Rule, or a religious command such as "Thou shalt not commit adultery."

Here is a list of personal sexual activities. On one side or the other of each item draw an arrow indicating whether *for you* the activity is to be placed toward the left as an aesthetic issue (a matter of taste) or toward the right as a moral issue (a matter of some other principle).

Aesthetic Issues   *Moral Issues*

Watching explicitly sexual movies
Sucking nipples
Engaging in premarital intercourse
Performing oral-genital sex
Engaging in extramarital intercourse
Masturbating
Using a vibrator for orgasm
Using contraceptives
Swimming at a nude beach
Forcing someone to have sex
Having sex with animals
Getting a sex-change operation
Having intercourse in the living room
Engaging in violent sex
Having an abortion
Engaging in anal intercourse
Using an item of clothing for sexual
    excitement
Participating in group sex
Having intercourse with a stranger
Having sex with a partner of the same sex
Having intercourse standing up
Taking money for sex
Seeking daily orgasms

If you have classed most of the items as aesthetic issues, your sexual choices are made largely in terms of your tastes or those with whom you are concerned. If you have classed all or most of the items as moral issues, your tendency is to make sexual choices on the basis of some yardstick other than taste. Shortly we shall consider what these yardsticks might be.

If you have a number of activities under each heading, then ponder what the basis for your distinction is. What do your moral issues have in common? What do activities you regard as matters of taste have in common? You may have had difficulty in making this judgment about certain items. Some are simple actions, such as sucking nipples, but others are a complex series of actions and relationships, such as premarital sex.

There are two good ways to test out your tastes when a sexual issue is at least partly a matter of taste for you. One is fantasy; the other is acting it out. Since fantasy is safer, it's a good place to start. If a sexual style seems to have some appeal, try it again and again in fantasy. A lot of what we yearn for sexually is pure fantasy. That's okay. You will enjoy the fantasy. If your fantasies confirm your interest in a sexual style, then you may wish to try it out. Of course, you don't have to jump from virginity into orgies. There are probably some tentative steps you can try out first. You may find some styles to be far more fun if they remain fantasies than if they are given flesh and bone.

Taste may be your primary way of evaluating a sexual style, whether your taste, your partner's taste, or your friends' or society's taste. Alternatively, taste may be simply one of many considerations that enter into your sexual behavior. After you decide what you like, and before you go on to act on your preference, you may consider one or another of the other ways of choosing.

Consequences: What If I Do It . . . ?

Probably most of us much of the time make our decisions with some thought for consequences. The question is, Which consequences?

From time immemorial the sexual rules of society have been enforced by fear of unwanted consequences, primarily pregnancy, venereal disease, and loss of reputation. In our time these dangers can be minimized by an alert individual, but they are still important considerations, since the incidence of both unwanted pregnancies and venereal disease continues to increase. Sex information becomes important primarily when you don't have it. If you are concerned with consequences at all, then you will want to stay abreast of the changing technical information in regard to contraception, abortion, and venereal disease. (The Bibliography is accompanied by a list of organizations that will be a continuing source of new information and assistance.)

Not all consequences, of course, are physical, nor are all unwanted. There are emotional consequences of sexual acts as well as physical, and pleasurable consequences as well as painful.

Three questions are usually uppermost in our minds when we consider consequences: (1) What are the possible results of a given choice? (2) How good or bad, pleasurable or painful, is each result? (3) How likely is each to happen? If the results seem both desirable and likely, then the choice usually presents little difficulty. We proceed. If the results seem extremely bad or are unlikely to offer any reward, then too the choice is usually easy. We don't proceed. Russian roulette is not a popular sport: while the chances are "only" one in six of getting killed, the risk is not worth taking, since the "reward" of living is available without playing the game.

Decision making is usually not so simple. Most often there are losses and gains. Some results are more likely to happen than others. The search for a course of action that maximizes good consequences and minimizes bad ones may involve tortuous hours of indecision.

Take Mary. She is very interested in Richard and realizes that he is also serious about her. He is attractive but quite conventional and seems rather tense about sex. There is every indication that he will go to the altar without ever going beyond a kiss and a warm embrace. At this point Mary has begun to worry that sex might prove to be a problem in their relationship. She is now considering taking the initiative herself and suggesting that they make love in order to explore their relationship further.

What consequences might Mary expect from suggesting intercourse? How good or bad is each? How likely is each? Here is the grid on which Mary evaluated the possible consequences of her plan.

Consequences Evaluation Grid

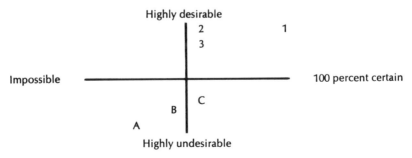

Mary saw three major benefits from her plan:

1. She could find out before marriage if she and Richard were sexually compatible. This she thinks is very desirable, since she could then avoid marriage if their sex life proved to be a disaster. As she is pretty sure Richard will agree to her proposal, she considers this consequence to be both fairly certain and highly desirable.

2. She would have more pleasure and less frustration if she and Richard have intercourse now. This too, she feels, is highly desirable, but she is less certain this will happen. In fact, she would never have considered this plan in the first place if she hadn't been worried about Richard's ability to give sexual pleasure. Thus, she gives this consequence only slightly over a 50–50 chance of occurring.

3. They would develop a closer relationship from having sex together. Since this would be a side benefit as far as Mary is concerned, she rates this consequence as slightly less desirable than the others but still as uncertain as 2.

At the same time Mary saw three main risks in her plan:

A. Richard might be shocked by such a proposal and leave her. This would upset her greatly. However, her knowledge of Richard leads her to believe that he will not leave. Thus, she considers this highly undesirable consequence to be unlikely as well.

B. Richard might not marry her if they had sex before marriage. Although she thinks Richard's intentions are likely to remain the same, Mary does see a somewhat greater risk in this undesirable consequence occurring.

C. Having sex now might rush things and produce less pleasure later. This Mary sees as the greatest danger to her plan. If she pushes Richard too hard or fast, disaster is quite likely to strike.

On the basis of this evaluation Mary decided to go ahead with her plan. She felt she could overcome her greatest risk if she made her suggestion but did not push Richard in carrying it out. If they proceeded slowly, later pleasure would not be forfeited, and there was a lot to be gained in finding out how their relationship would really work.

If you wish to consider consequences carefully, you can use the evaluation grid to organize your thinking. List the major advantages you see in a style you are considering, and plot them on the grid. How desirable is each? How likely to happen? Then list the major disadvantages you see. How desirable is each? How likely to happen? Plot them on the grid. If you are considering more than one style, do a new grid for each style.

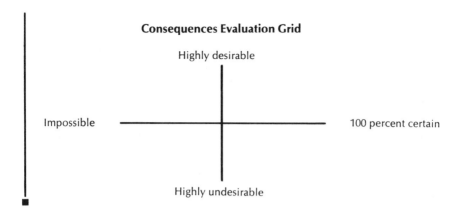

By this point you may be dismayed by all this scheming and calculating. After all, evaluating consequences is only one way of making sexual choices. You may wonder what has happened to freedom, spontaneity, and the mystery of human emotions. Calculation may seem to destroy the artistry of sex. Or you may be shaking your head ruefully and saying, "Doesn't anyone do anything just because it's *right* anymore? What has happened to moral rules and principles?"

As we discussed the matter of taste and the question of consequences, we did not ask, Whose taste, or consequences for whom? We can make those decisions entirely as personal judgments: "All that matters is what I prefer." Or, "All that I consider are the consequences that affect me. However, if other people act that way, my taste and the consequences that affect me would be left out of their consideration." Even self-interest requires concern for the interests of others. We tend to universalize our judgments: we do unto others as we would have them do unto us. This is yet another way of making sexual choices.

However, using reason to universalize by itself may not tell you what to do. Bernard Shaw has one of his characters say, "Do not do unto others as you would they should do unto you. Their taste may not be the same." Does your sexual partner like to be stimulated in exactly the same places you do? Often the rule is more useful in its negative form: do nothing to anyone that you would not want to be done to you. Thus, the rule may not tell you what to do, but it may raise warning signals when you are in danger of acting unreasonably as if you are the only person who matters. Do you ever pursue a sexual behavior because you would like your partner to do the same? Do you ever refrain from doing something sexual because you would not like your partner to do the same?

Universalizing Sex: "Do unto Others . . ."

Selfishness is an issue that you may consider seriously in the handling of sexual choices. If I pursue my personal wishes alone, I am in danger of using my sexual partner as a means to my ends. If I focus only on my orgasm, my partner may become a tool or toy for my enjoyment. Similarly, viewing sex primarily as the means to having children may make both partners exploited tools in the pursuit of this social goal.

On the other hand, not many of us like to have someone else always taking care of us, constantly doing things just to be nice, never claiming anything for themselves. Usually there is some kind of price to be extracted by such behavior. It is demeaning to be a constant object of charity. Sex can be dissatisfying if your partner is always trying to give you a good time without mutual enjoyment. There is a subtle medley of self-indulgence and indulgence of the other person that provides the magic of sexual delight. If the mix has too much self, the result is exploitation. If there is too much effort to please, the result is philanthropy. In either case, delight is diminished.

These considerations may seem very abstract and unrelated to your concrete situation. One way to simplify the matter is by asking yourself, "Am I using other people only as tools or objects for my own gratification, or do I value them in their own right?" Thus, you may be seeing a partner merely as a means to a "good lay" or, for that matter, a way to produce a baby. Or you may be enjoying the other person in the uniqueness of their being and worth. The question can also be turned around: "Am I allowing other people to use me as a tool or object for their own gratification, or do they value me in my own right?"

The importance you give to your own and other people's interests fundamentally affects your choice of sexual style. This is not a simple question of right and wrong: it is right to consider others and wrong not to. Rather, self-concern is a basic ingredient in your concern for others and concern for others is an ingredient in concern for yourself. The real issue is what the blend is that gives meaning to your sexual existence.

Authority: "Help! I Need Some Good Advice"

When you make sexual choices, especially when you reflect on the sexual style you wish to pursue, you no doubt consider the opinions of others. There are countless authorities you might consult to help you make your decisions: parents, friends, priest, doctor, sex expert, and so on. You may welcome the judgments of some and fear the judgments of others.

It is sometimes surprising to find who the authorities really are who influence us. A certain group of young friends talked frequently about casual sex, usually in a joking way. But behind the palaver was the obvious assumption that casual sex is a forbidden pleasure. If they should ever find one of their number "fooling around," that person would be dropped immediately. The authority of the peer group often pressures behavior in one direction or another. You may welcome or resent this pressure. Conforming to the group may give you a sense of "belongingness" or it may feel stifling.

The choice of which authorities you will heed is an important one. This is not only a matter of whether you will obey the authority of religion or the voices of science. You may listen to both. It is also a question of which religious tradition and which scientific perspective, since they do not all agree.

Today the diversity of judgment among religious sects is hardly less varied than that within the population at large. There are very liberal, even radical, views that refuse to condemn homosexuality, extramarital intercourse, and a variety of other sexual acts formerly prohibited by religious authority. Instead, they suggest that the circumstances, purposes, and probable results of these behaviors have to be considered to make moral judgments. Even within the religious groups that support the traditional Judeo-Christian emphasis on strictly monogamous sexual activity within marriage, there is a range of opinion. Some religious authorities wish to retain the specific rules of the traditional code. Others wish only to affirm the time-honored values of sexual fidelity within marriage. Still others want to retain the primary value of monogamy while refraining from judgment on the specific ways by which this may be carried out. There is enough disagreement even on the conservative side of these questions to leave the seeker the serious task of deciding which authorities to follow.[1]

If you are a member of a faith that exerts strong moral authority, then very clear sexual guidance may be provided through rules of behavior. Your religious tradition has very likely taken a position on the style you are considering right now. If your faith condemns a style you prefer, you may face an either/or choice between your religion and your preferred style. On the other hand, you may have a somewhat flexible religious commitment and then another quandary emerges: a tension between personal conviction and the religious authority. Imagine your sexual values to be a rubber band. How far will the rubber band stretch? If it snaps, what do you do then? Do you go with your religious authority or your independent moral judgment? What is then likely to happen?

The authority of religion is not always vested in rules of behavior. Some will understand it to be moral guidance subject to change with new information and a changing moral climate. In that case, the strain will not be so acute, although there is likely to remain a tension between individual judgment and the judgments common in the religious group.

Still other sources of authority are the experts, specialists in one field or another who make judgments about sexual style. You may want to know current medical judgment about abortion or pregnancy or about the effectiveness or dangers of different methods of contraception. Or you may want to consult current psychological research about homosexuality. Certainly it is good to make informed judgments. Much human misery has been the product of ignorance and misinformation about things sexual and relational. But facts alone do not make decisions. For example, there is minimal risk to the physical health of a woman who has a medically supervised abortion during the first three months of pregnancy. This fact is essential for a woman considering an abortion. But few women make this decision on the basis of such facts alone. Religious authority, personal preference, emotional consequences, economic situation, and a host of other factors are likely to enter into such a decision.

Who are the authorities you consider in making sexual decisions? Suppose you had to choose your sexual style by this time tomorrow, that you had just twenty-four hours to make your decision. How would you spend the time between now and then? Note how many hours you would spend doing each of the following:

1. Talking to others:

_____ Partner   _____ Family doctor

_____ Friends   _____ Counselor or therapist

_____ Parents   _____ Sex expert

_____ Religious adviser   _____ Other

2. Reading books or articles written by:

_____ Medical experts

_____ Marriage or family counselors

_____ Psychologists

_____ Pastoral counselors (religious)

_____ Others

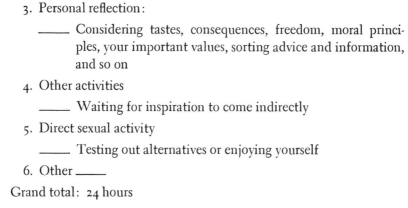

3. Personal reflection:

_____ Considering tastes, consequences, freedom, moral principles, your important values, sorting advice and information, and so on

4. Other activities

_____ Waiting for inspiration to come indirectly

5. Direct sexual activity

_____ Testing out alternatives or enjoying yourself

6. Other _____

Grand total: 24 hours

Now that you have looked at all the ways you might make your decision, which ones are actually important to you? On page 116 is a chart that outlines most of the questions you can ask yourself when choosing a sexual style. Outline heavily the boxes containing the questions that seem most relevant to you in the choice or choices you are currently facing. Cross out any questions that you do not want or need to consider. Thinking about each question will be helpful, but you will find it more useful if you actually jot down some answers to the questions you deem most important.

Style Evaluation Chart

	Personal concerns	Relational concerns	Social concerns
Destiny	How free am I to pursue this style?	How free is my partner to consider this?	Does society pressure me to accept or reject this style?
Taste	What are my likes and dislikes?	What are my partner's likes and dislikes?	Are there any preferences in my community that I wish to consider?
Consequence	What are the advantages and disadvantages to me?	What are the advantages and disadvantages to our relationship?	Are there advantages and disadvantages to society in general?
Universalizing reason	Do I want this style for my sake only? Would I be willing to exchange places with anyone else involved in this style?	Do we want this for the sake of our relationship only or also for the sake of others as well?	What if everyone pursued this style?
Authority — Moral and religious	What moral or religious rules do I wish to consider?	What moral or religious rules are important to our relationship?	What moral or religious rules are important to society?
Authority — Family or society	What might my family or peers feel or do about my acting out this style?	What might our families or peers feel or do about us as a couple pursuing this style?	Does society impose any legal rules upon us concerning this style?
Authority — Expert opinion	What judgments by medical or psychological experts about this style do I wish to consider?	What judgments by medical or psychological experts about this style are important to our relationship?	What judgments by experts do I wish to consider about the social value of this style?

11

Pigeonholes

A party was in full swing. You were introduced to this person, John/ Mary . . . you can't remember now. The two of you exchanged a few words and danced together briefly. Later you were in conversation with an old friend when your eyes met those of your new acquaintance from across the room. You knew instantly what the look in those eyes meant. Your head made some quick calculations and out popped the conclusion: "He/she is not for me."

New people cross your path daily, perhaps hourly. If you were to consider seriously each one as a possible sexual partner, even in fantasy, you would soon go mad. You would have no time to think of anything else! Instead, you simplify the process with a certain bureaucratic efficiency. You think, "That person is too young, too old, too married, too male, too female, too weak, too strong, too hot, too cold, too aggressive, too passive, too ugly, too beautiful, too gay, too straight, too fat, too thin, too rough, too smooth. . . ." Or you think, "I'm too young, too old, too married, . . ."

These thoughts are ways of organizing your sexual feelings and expressing your values. You accept or reject the possibility of a sexual advance or even a sexual fantasy by putting yourself and others into sexual pigeonholes.

Often sexual pigeonholes are not very sexy. These snap judgments usually express negative feelings: "He's a smooth operator. I can't stand men like that." "She's a real seductress. She scares me." They are "stop action" statements that protect the speaker from sexual involvement. They can, and often do, represent a callous disregard for the uniqueness of the other person.

Mike Macho
"Look at my muscles! One look at me makes them swoon."

Mr. Important
"I'm too busy for this sex stuff!"

Hal Pless
"Please! I need someone like you to take care of me."

Sym Bios
"I'll rub yours if you do mine."

Peter Potent
"I can get it off anywhere, anytime."

Big Daddy
"Be my baby! I'll take care of you."

Tyrone Technique
"A smooth line and a deft hand gets me what I want."

Mac Sadd
"You really like it when I hurt you."

Earthmother
"I'll take care of your every need."

Flora Fluff
"Come on, handsome, you can't resist my feminine charm."

Diana Distance
"Don't you dare touch me!"

Laura Layaway
"You can do it to me if you want to."

Fanny Free
"Let's get it on! I don't just fool around."

Sally Soph
"A woman of the world gets the 'man about town.'"

Tina Touché
"Go away, closer. Hands off, love me a whole lot."

Ida Ignor
"I don't know *what* you're talking about."

Nevertheless, some classification of others is not only inevitable; it may be desirable. Indeed, classification of oneself may be an important part of understanding yourself. Therefore, a look at the way you use sexual stereotypes, how you caricature yourself and others, can be revealing.

On page 118 are some cartoons exaggerating sexual images. There are eight pigeonholes representing male styles and eight representing female styles. Actually, several of the caricatures work for either sex. Both pictures and statements are caricatures, and like most caricatures, they are negative, even when there is subtle affection expressed. Ponder them unhurriedly.

Now choose two or three that best represent the exaggeration of images you most often project. Which image best represents you? Do you feel yourself getting defensive? "I don't act like any of those, ever!" That's okay. If you don't feel defensive, chances are none of them represents you. A good way to clarify which one is most like you is to see which one makes you most uncomfortable or apologetic about yourself.

Now look for the cartoon images your partner or partners project. Ask yourself, "Which of these images works best on me?" Choose the two or three you feel are most effective when used on you. Again, your own defensive feelings may be a clue to your reactions. Now consider which of the cartoon images represents the sexual approach that you dislike most and that works least well in getting your cooperation.

If you're really brave, draw a cartoon of yourself as a sexual person. None of those provided really fits you, does it? Try drawing a cartoon that exaggerates the image you project with more precision. You don't have to show it to anybody. If drawing is your problem, simply use triangles and circles to depict your figures, like this:

Mike Macho   **Mr. Important**   **Earthmother**

Give yourself a name, and write a sentence or two that caricatures the sexual image you project. Can you laugh about it? Is it too painful to be funny?

These caricatures usually function best to tell you whom you *don't* want to get involved with, what style you want to resist. They tell you whom you *do* wish to get involved with only in the gross sense of identifying the groups you don't feel negative about. You might encounter dozens of people who fit your desired categories before you find someone with whom you really want more sexual involvement. The reason is simple: stereotypes are painted with a broad brush. They do not detail the subtle differences between people or the mysterious chemistry that develops between persons—sometimes quite contrary to stereotypical expectations.

In a relationship of depth and permanence, relying on stereotypes can be disastrous: "You're such a cold fish. No wonder we never have sex." "You're so busy, I have to make an appointment a week in advance to have sex—and then you only give me fifteen minutes." Changes of mood and circumstances are the only sources of spontaneity and novelty for a monogamous couple. To put one's partner into a "no sex" pigeonhole is to reject sex for oneself.

Changes in values, in emotional character, in physical functioning, take place over the years. To act on the basis of a fixed understanding of what a partner is like is to live with an outdated fantasy rather than a real partner. Stereotypes that work so efficiently in some situations can also squeeze out the human dynamic when it is needed. When you consider the caricatures you use, who is most often unjustly treated: yourself, your partner, or your nonpartners?

Sex in Silver and Gray

The previous stereotypes are based on matters of personality and choice. There are other classifications supposedly based on physical fact. You are either male or female, twenty or sixty. People are not confused by these differences: they are not likely to relate to a woman as if she were a man or to children as if they were adults. Nevertheless, there is a variety of ways of being male or female, and there are many ways of being young or elderly. We recognize these variations in most areas of life but are remarkably reluctant to recognize them sexually.

For those between twenty and sixty a substantial number of pigeonholes is provided. There is "Sex for the ambitious young man," "Sex for the career girl," "Sex for the married woman," "Sex for the college dropout," "Sex for the successful executive." At both ends of the age spectrum the pigeonholes are fewer, the choices less broad. Instead, society tends to say, "No sex, please, you're too young," or "No sex, please, you're too old."

The stereotype pretends that children are nonsexual and that youths are less sexual than they are. The innocence of the little child is too beguiling to allow one to imagine that erections, secretions, and pleasant genital touching are going on. But they are. The intense sexual feelings of young people are ignored by a moral system that expects of all what only a few can manage. The fact that youths so largely refuse to be placed in the pigeonholes their elders wish for them is no doubt the result of the relentless power of sexual impulses.

With age it is a different matter. The feelings are not so powerful, the urge not so unrelenting. So when society says to older people, "Be sexless!" vast numbers comply, slipping meekly into their pigeonholes and unhappily looking out at those who still enjoy the satisfactions of sexual intimacy.

Here is a quiz to check out how much your attitudes conform to presently available facts about sex for the aging. Circle *T* if you know or think the statement is true, *F* if you think it is false. Answer every question, even if you have to guess.

T F 1. A man who is heterosexual all his life will never get involved in homosexual relations at age sixty-five.

T F 2. Over half of unmarried women between fifty and seventy continue to masturbate.

T F 3. One-fourth of men masturbate after age sixty-five.

T F 4. An older man has some advantage over a younger man in sexual intercourse, since he has much better control of ejaculation.

T F 5. The older man may require several minutes of sexual stimulation, while only a few seconds are usually required for a younger man to reach a strong erection.

T F 6. The loss of the ability to have an erection is not to be expected as a natural part of the aging process.

T F 7. Men invariably lose their potency after prostate surgery. Women always lose sexual interest after a hysterectomy (surgical removal of the uterus).

T F 8. A woman's sexual desire continues largely undiminished until she is sixty or older.

T F 9. Nearly half of all men between the ages of seventy-five and ninety-two experience satisfying coitus.

T F 10. Seven out of ten married couples over age sixty remain sexually active.

T   F   11. About 70 percent of married women aged sixty continue to have intercourse with their husbands.

T   F   12. More than one in ten of sixty-year-old women who no longer have husbands continue to experience coitus.

T   F   13. Vaginal lubrication takes ten to thirty seconds of sexual stimulation in younger women but may take one to three minutes in older women.

T   F   14. After menopause the vaginal walls become thinner and less resilient, and this condition increases gradually with age. In some women this may cause coitus to be uncomfortable unless hormones are replaced medicinally.

T   F   15. There is no physiological reason why the frequency of sexual expression that a woman finds satisfying in her earlier years should not be carried over into her postmenopausal sexual style.

All but two of the foregoing statements are true, according to current research opinion. You might like to go back over the statements to see if you can identify the two that are false, and then look in the footnote to check your answers.[1] (The footnote is on page 178.) Unless you have read widely in the literature of sex research, you probably will have been surprised by some of these statements. We cannot outline this vast research here, but the following facts are important to know. Otherwise you may find you are stuffing yourself or other people into the wrong pigeonholes.

1. Satisfying sexual activity may go on into the eighties and beyond. As long as a person of either sex is in good health and has the opportunity for regular genital contact, there is no biological reason to expect sexual interest or response to cease.

2. With age, sexual response slows down and the intensity of orgasm decreases. Sexual response follows the same course as all physiological functions. Just as you would not expect to run the four-minute mile at age eighty, so you should not expect to be a champion of the "quickie." You can still walk the mile and enjoy the exercise if you are in good health, and you can still enjoy an orgasm. In both cases it just takes longer. Whereas people expect their sight, hearing, and strength to decline with age, they often forget that sexual response will also decline. Thus, they panic at the first sign of the sexual slowdown. This can create problems, but these are usually caused by mental anxiety, not by physical incapacity.

3. Female sexual interest tends to be high in middle age and may even

increase at menopause. This is probably the result of emotional factors such as fewer family responsibilities or no fear of pregnancy. The hormonal changes after menopause do not reduce sexual interest unless and until the imbalance becomes extreme enough to produce discomfort in intercourse or orgasm. This may not happen at all, and in fact, intercourse is enjoyed by many women after the seventieth year.

4. Male sexual interest and response decrease only gradually as physical stamina declines. In older men erections occur less frequently and less vigorously, orgasm takes longer, and the ejaculate is thinner. None of these need negate sexual pleasure. But the anxiety produced by erective or ejaculatory slowness may produce performance anxieties. Psychic factors such as retirement anxiety, fear of aging, or personal habits of overeating or drinking are more apt to reduce the sexual enjoyment of the aging male.

5. The need and desire for affection and personal intimacy is unaffected by age. If the loss of sexual intimacy is not replaced by other forms of intimacy, personal loneliness is apt to be intense and painful.

6. People who maintain an active sex life retain their sexual prowess with little or no impairment.[2] This may or may not be a causal connection. But the implication seems to be, "Use it, or you'll lose it!"

These various statements, supported by current research, indicate that the sexual pigeonholes into which aging people are placed do not conform well to the facts of biology nor to the behavior of many older people. To be sure, the choices open to the elderly are more limited than those available to younger people. But families and society limit the options still more. Is it necessary for every nursing or retirement home to stuff the elderly into pigeonholes labeled "No Sex, Please—You're Aged"? Could different or roomier pigeonholes be made?

This problem becomes more and more acute as the life span increases and the extended family in which older members once had a place disappears. Your chances of living into your eighth decade are very good, and the possibility of remaining healthy and active is good as well. You will have time on your hands after sixty-five, without a job and with fewer responsibilities. You may discover that others do not respect you as fully as they once did. You may not respect yourself as much. Your financial situation may be restrictive. You will almost certainly experience the loss of friends. Your partner may die before you and probably will if you are female. You are unlikely to live with your children. Isolation and loneliness are distinct possibilities.

So how do you wish to live sexually in your later years? If sex has been either a duty or an anxiety for you, you may welcome the fact that you are no longer expected to respond or perform sexually. You may wish to rest from sex, just as you rest from work. If so, the sexless stereotypes to which you are expected to conform are not so much a problem as a solution to what may have been a lifelong tension. Even if your sexual existence was generally satisfying, you may still welcome a time of life in which all the drives and pressures are reduced and your existence can assume a relaxed and mellow contentment.

However, for many people this expectation is a cage, a barrier against intimate human contact, continued vibrancy, and sexual expressiveness. You may welcome the relief from duty, not in order to rest, but in order to have time for your partner and other people. You may hope that your sexual enjoyment will not cease but that you will find ways to continue sexual excitement. You may want less sex but not less satisfying sex.

If so, there is good news from the laboratories of sex researchers: lots of people do it, and probably you can, too. You may have to overcome the conspiracy abroad to make you think you can't "get it off" anymore. But you can mount a counterconspiracy to find ways to relate intimately and sexually. You may be able to get beyond the artificial taboos and restrictions that romanticize sex as the private possession of the young. If it is a self-fulfilling expectation that age is sexless, it can be a self-fulfilling prophecy that the later years provide their own style of sexual enjoyment. The quickie may be out, but leisurely sex is not. If you are young but hope for a sexy old age, perhaps you want to join now in tearing down the signs that say, "No Sex, Please—You're Aged."

Putting "Male" and "Female" in Their Place

You may not act the way your father or mother did, but you still surely carry around a vision of how you should behave sexually as male or female. Society provides pigeonholes for men and pigeonholes for women. As fast as one is destroyed, a new one seems to be put in its place. Remember the seduction scenarios in Chapter 5? Some relied on old images of what it means to be male or female, while others made use of new ones. But regardless of whether you are seen as "Papa's Ideal Girl" or "A Liberated Woman," you are still pressured to conform to a stereotype.

The stereotypes with which you live as male or female may be very useful and comfortable to you, providing the security and routine you desire. However, just like the stereotypes of aging, these expectations may feel like a cage restricting your movement. They may make it difficult or even impossible for you to have satisfying sexual contacts.

As with age pigeonholes, sex pigeonholes rest upon what we assume to be the facts of sexual functioning.

Here is a quiz to check out your understanding of these facts in relation to present research. Circle the *T* before statements you know or guess to be true. Circle *F* before false statements.

T F 1. Men's sexual interest peaks in their twenties; women's interest peaks in their thirties.

T F 2. Only about 7 percent of males are capable of more than one orgasm within the space of a few minutes, and practically all of these males are young men.

T F 3. Female physiology makes possible multiple orgasms; that is, successive orgasms can follow immediately when stimulation is continued.

T F 4. Many normal women feel unsatisfied with just one orgasm.

T F 5. Half or more of all women have nocturnal orgasms at some time or another.

T F 6. There is no physiological difference between an orgasm produced by stimulation of the clitoris and that produced by stimulation of the vagina.

T F 7. Women will experience their most physiologically intense orgasm and are more certain of having an orgasm when stimulation is from masturbation.

T F 8. Women generally are more oriented to the emotional factors in sexual enjoyment than men. They will therefore usually enjoy orgasm more in coition than in masturbation.

T F 9. Three-fourths of all men ejaculate within two minutes of intromission (insertion of the penis into the vagina).

T F 10. Orgasmic women usually need ten to twenty minutes after intromission for orgasm to occur.

T F 11. Men who enjoy stimulation of their nipples have suppressed homosexual desires.

T F 12. Oral-genital sexual enjoyment between men and women indicates homosexual tendencies.

T F 13. The size of the male penis is a significant factor in the enjoyment of sexual intercourse for the man or the woman, or both.

T F 14. The penis ordinarily rubs directly on the clitoris during intercourse, thus providing the stimulation the woman needs for orgasm.

T   F   15. Since sexual enjoyment is so largely emotional, it is ideal
            for the man and the woman to have simultaneous orgasms.

Once again it is important to sort out fact from fallacy. Otherwise you
may be expecting the impossible from yourself or your sexual partner. A
stereotype that opposes physiology is bound to lead to frustration. Therefore, let us tell you that the first ten statements are true; the last five false.[3]

The stereotype that labels women as less adequate sexually than men
is not accurate, but it is easy to see from the quiz how it has arisen. Men
do achieve orgasm much more quickly than do women (although the
gap lessens with age). Although the clitoris is the place of greatest sexual
sensitivity in women, it is not stimulated directly by the penis during intercourse, but only indirectly by pressure and the pulling of the folds of the
surrounding tissue. Female orgasm is not as specifically focused in one
place as the male's is in the penis. A greater range of emotional and social
factors is involved in female sexual response.

What the stereotype ignores is that very few men even at the height of
their sexual capacity are able to have more than one orgasm in a short
space of time. They need a "recovery" period before an erection becomes
possible again. By contrast, many women can have two, three, or more
orgasms in quick succession. Female sexual response does not require a
recovery period. In terms of sheer number of orgasms possible, women
are far more "sexual" than men.

Many male and female stereotypes have effectively blocked or reduced
sexual enjoyment. Men have been labeled as "dominant." "aggressive," "initiating." Women have been labeled "submissive," "passive," "compliant."
As the initiator, the dominant one, the man ends up on top in intercourse.
In this position his needs are quickly met, but not so likely the woman's.
Women cannot easily control the stimulation that suits them best in this
position. It is the position with the female on top that most often results
in orgasm for women. Yet a woman who feels it is not "nice" to ask for
what she wants, who always is passive or submissive, may never experience
a position of intercourse that is satisfying to her. If they cannot shed the
stereotypes, a couple may not discover other positions of intercourse that
could be satisfying to both of them.

If a "big deal" is not made of it, a man who wants to can ordinarily
learn to slow down his orgasm and to achieve greater satisfaction for himself and his partner. If the stereotypes are not too much in control, the
male can wait until the female is sufficiently aroused and give full attention
to the movements and stimulations that will most likely produce her
orgasm. Then they can both give full attention to the stimulations that

will make his orgasm most satisfying. The pitfall to watch for here is the temptation to "try too hard" to orchestrate the perfect orgasmic experience.

Some women seldom achieve orgasm in intercourse. Even women who are sexually very responsive and have a regular partner achieve orgasm in only about 75 percent of their coital contacts. This does not mean women are less sexual than men but that intercourse does not provide the stimulation that is ideal for the female orgasm. Masturbation, as we have noted, is much more certain to produce orgasm for women. But other taboos may prevent a couple from lovingly and mutually engaging in the manual stimulation needed to satisfy the woman.

Moreover, the woman is prepared for the nonfulfillment of her sexual needs by an upbringing that says this is the way it should be. The result is that she may be quite satisfied with her nonsatisfaction. The same process that builds the pigeonholes also provides the expectations that enable one to live in them.

You cannot simply junk the stereotypes, whether they are based on fact or fantasy. The man who has internalized the image of being hot and horny all the time cannot some afternoon change to a responsive and co-equal lover. The woman who sees herself as possessing sexuality only to please a man will not one day utter a mating cry and drag her man off to bed. The issue is, as usual, What are the things you might want to change, and of these, which are realistic possibilities?

Think that over. If the stereotype feels good for you and for those with whom you are sexually involved, there is no serious problem. Is that true for you? Does the cartoon you drew of yourself merely exaggerate characteristics you are quite happy to have? Or are there at least a few things you would like to change about your sexual image? Would you like that pigeonhole to be a little roomier?

You could experiment a bit with different styles of behavior. This does not mean you should become a Jekyll-Hyde character. Rather, try out in small and sensitive ways what it might be like to move out of the typical role and manner by which you relate sexually. Such experimentation does not require a regular sexual partner, although if you do have one, you can have a lot of fun talking about, and trying out, new behaviors with each other. You may find that some new way of relating really suits you better, or you may be glad to climb back into your old box. Remember, though, almost anything seems strange the first time.

Pigeonholes can be comfy nests or confining cages. Which they are usually depends on whether they are entered willingly or not. May "your place" be roomy enough for comfort and comfortable enough for a long-term stay.

12

Communicating Your Sexual Style

Jane thinks that Dick thinks that she is not very sexy. So tonight she really lets go. Dick responds, "Wow, are you a sizzler!" Jane thinks, "Now he's making fun of me," and she turns off.

Dick says to Jane in anguish, "I can't seem to locate your clitoris." Jane says to Dick, "I'm sure I put it back between my legs when I used it last."

Dick says to Jane, "Let's go to bed early." Translation: "I want to make love." Jane says to Dick, "Okay by me; I'd like to read my book." Translation: "I don't want to make love, so I'll ignore your fuzzy message."

Dick says to Jane, "Jill has nice breasts, doesn't she?" Jane says to Dick, "I never notice such things; you're the connoisseur." Jane thinks, "Dick doesn't like my breasts." Dick thinks, "Jane isn't interested in sex."

Jane says to Dick, "Oh, that feels good." Dick says to Jane, "What feels good?" Jane: "What you're doing feels good." Dick: "What am I doing?" Jane: "Oh, you know. . . ."

Such are the perils of sexual communication.

Communication is a skill. You can learn and practice how to send and receive clearer messages. However, communication is also a choice.

Since before you learned to talk, you have been choosing what and how much to tell and to whom. You have also been deciding to what and to whom to listen and when to tune out. Among the important choices that go into your sexual styles are those that determine what kind of communicator you will be.

There is good evidence that better communication means better sex. In a magazine survey to which more than 100,000 women replied, 88 percent of the women who reported that they always discussed sexual desires and feelings with their husbands also reported good or very good sexual satisfaction. At the same time, 70 percent of those who said they never discussed these matters reported fair or poor sex lives.[1] Moreover, improving communication skill is central to the sex therapy developed by Masters and Johnson. The implication seems to be this: if you want good sex, then talk about it. Even if you don't want sex, good or otherwise, you may need to talk your way out of other people's plans for you.

The Sounds of Silence

Sex talk is hard for all of us some of the time and for some of us it is hard any time. It may not be easy to say directly what we feel, think, want. Yet the irony is that what we don't say, as well as what we do say, sends a message. Silence can be as noisy as a shout.

Ron and Paula have been together about five years. Ron would like to ask Paula to study a sex book with him to put some spice into their languishing sex. Each time he has "chickened out." After all, Paula had a very sheltered upbringing. She would be horrified at such a suggestion, to say nothing of her reaction to trying what such a book might suggest. Expressions like "dirty old man" and "porno freak" flash through his mind every time he imagines the scene.

Paula for her part has noticed that Ron is not as happy as he once was. Wondering if she has done something to offend him, she has taken up every signal from Ron about when or how to make love just to "prove" that she really loves him. Sometimes she thinks putting her desire to please Ron before her own desires has resulted in rather mechanical sex. She has thought of telling Ron this, but he always seems uncomfortable when they get near the subject. So she has decided to stay clear of sex in any discussion. If Ron is unhappy with their sex life, he would be even more upset if she confessed her own unhappiness.

Ron sees Paula's mechanical behavior as discomfort with sex itself, rather than discomfort with his discomfort. This shows that he was right in the first place not to bring up the subject of sex. This leads to more unhappiness on his part, which leads to more discomfort on Paula's part, which leads to . . . and so on, around and around.

Sounds complicated, doesn't it? Actually it is a very common pattern in sexual relationships. How many times have you heard or said, "I can't tell her that. She'd murder me!" Or, "I think he thinks I'm frigid/seductive/bossy. . . ." The sexual meaning may be clear; it may be deeply buried. R. D. Laing has written an entertaining, but grimly true, little book of verses called *Knots,* which unravels a variety of spirals that snarl communication:

> There is something I don't know
>   that I am supposed to know.
> I don't know what it is I don't know,
>   and yet am supposed to know,
> and I feel I look stupid
>   if I seem both not to know it
>   and not know *what* it is I don't know.
> Therefore I pretend to know everything.
>
> I feel you know what I am supposed to know
> but you can't tell me what it is
> because you don't know that I don't know what it is.
>
> You may know what I don't know, but not
>   that I don't know it,
> and I can't tell you. So you will have to
>   tell me everything.[2]

Can you remember a time when you were sexually involved with a person and either pretended to know what you did not know or failed to say what you knew you wanted? What message did your partner receive from this noncommunication? Is this what you wanted to be received?

If you cannot remember such a time, recall any recent interchange with a sexual partner or prospective partner. Did you communicate what you intended? Did the communication help your relationship, or did it leave one or the other of you feeling hurt or angry?

Ground Control to Dick and Jane

Dick and Jane are sexual communications centers. They each send out signals, verbal and nonverbal, and they each receive signals. They choose styles of communication. Jane may choose to send out very few signals or she may choose to send out frequent, even constant, signals, loud and clear. That is the question of sexual openness, whether with Dick or with the rest of the world. Dick can tune his antennae carefully to sense every little sexual wave in the air, or he may prefer to receive only loud and obvious messages. That is the question of sexual listening. Both Dick and Jane make both of these kinds of choices. Obviously, either of them can jam communication. This may be accidental, a result of the lack of skill. It can also be on purpose, the result either of malice or of good intentions.

The choices for Dick and Jane are complicated by the fact that they were handed a garbled message in the first place. When they were little, adults told them to tell the truth: "It's a sin to tell a lie." However, they also received a second message, whether from padded shoulders and slimming girdles or from "fish stories" and "little white lies": "The truth can hurt too much." This double message complicates communication. Now if Dick decides to tell Jane how he honestly feels, she will be hurt and he will feel bad because he hurt her. If he decides not to tell her because she will be hurt, he feels bad because he was not honest. The question is not simply whether Dick is being open and honest with Jane. More basically, Dick is choosing and developing a way of communication that is more or less well suited to the values he holds dear.

Just like Dick and Jane, you must decide what you are going to say and to whom on the basis of your values. Is honesty an important principle you wish to follow? Sometimes? Always? Probably trying to be absolutely honest is absurd. A person who tells the whole truth at every moment is a good definition of a blabbermouth. So you decide how honest to be in a given situation. Some things you don't say because they are unnecessarily hurtful. Then, should you be honest only when it will foster love or some other value more basic for you? Or is it necessary to risk hurt and anger for yourself or for someone else because of the value of honesty and what honesty secures?

Earlier we looked at some of the questions surrounding openness about "outside sex." However, similar issues beset any sexual style. Here are a few examples: Is it okay to talk to a third person about a sexual problem you and your partner have? Will you tell your family about your sexual style when you think they will be offended by it? Should you reveal your sexual style if you think you will be discriminated against because of it? Would you do this over your partner's objections? The most important questions about openness and honesty are those between sexual partners: in casual sex, deciding what you tell a temporary partner; in procreative sex, talking out a decision to have children; in relational sex, negotiating the sexual terms of the relationship; in expressive sex, tuning in to each other's erotic desires. You can spell out the questions that are most crucial to your sexual existence.

What are your patterns of openness and honesty? Below are some "intimacy orbits" expanding out from you. On the left are your personal contacts. On the right are professional contacts. Delete, change, or move any to fit your situation. (For example, if you do not have a lover, you may wish to put a female friend there and a male friend in the other "good friend" slot. Or you may want to move "work colleague" out to the farthest orbit.) In any case, put the contacts you feel closest to in the orbits nearest to yourself and the ones you feel most distant from in the farthest orbits.

Then look at the list of things you might reveal to someone. Place the letter of each item in the orbits of the person or persons with whom you would share that particular information. Those things you would tell no one, place in the circle marked "self."

Intimacy Orbits

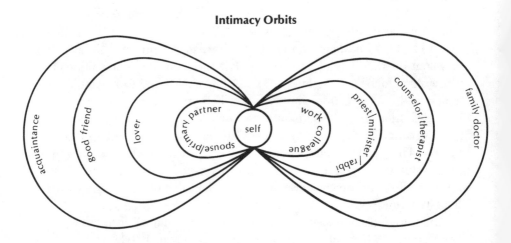

To whom would you tell the following?

     a. I like what you are wearing.

     b. I do not like what you are wearing.

     c. I am having an affair.

     d. I don't like oral-genital contact.

     e. I am dissatisfied with my sex life.

     f. I think you do not like me.

     g. I find you physically attractive.

     h. I find you physically unattractive.

     i. I like oral-genital contact.

     j. I think your sexual style is irresponsible.

     k. I think you think I am cold or distant.

     l. My partner and I have a sexual problem.

What determines when you wish to be honest or open about something? Very likely you did not want to be open or honest about all these things with people in every orbit. You may have felt that there would be no point in telling a casual acquaintance that you do not like his or her coat, whereas you would tell your partner this. Your partner might be hurt but might listen to you and appreciate knowing your feelings. On the other hand, perhaps you felt such an issue not important enough to your well-being to justify the hurt your partner would feel from such criticism.

Are you more or less honest with people who are more distant from you? You may find you are willing to discuss a sexual problem you and your partner have with a professional adviser, whereas revealing such matters to a mutual friend would be breaking trust. On the other hand, you may feel that this is what friendship is all about, being helpfully available to one another. Do you find yourself talking about such matters to complete strangers on an airplane or in a bar? This can at times be useful and free-ing, but not talking to your partner while regularly talking to strangers can be an attempt to relieve the pressures without facing the difficulty.

When Words Misbehave

You may have remembered a time or two when you were forthright in one of the situations in the exercise, not because you were really trying to be honest, but because you were angry at the other person and wanted to "get back" at him or her. Using honesty as a disguise for malice is a great temptation. Fear of anger sometimes causes strange behavior. Some people cry rather than show anger or laugh to stifle an angry snarl. If you know you are fearful of anger, watch out for your "honest remarks." Your honesty may have more to do with slashing your partner than revealing the truth: "I hate to tell you this, but you look ten years older than you are."

Honesty may be used for other ulterior motives as well. To illustrate, a man may feel guilty about an affair he has been having, so he tells his wife about it, assures her he really loves only her, and asks her forgiveness. She forgives him, and everything goes along smoothly for a while. At length he finds himself involved with another woman. Once more the guilt and tension from secret meetings get too much for him. With remorse he confesses what he has done. Once again she forgives him. The husband gets rid of his guilt by "telling all" to his wife. When she forgives him, he is relieved from his unhappy feelings and of his responsibility for his actions. Honesty is not really the issue. Would he not be better off if he worked through his conflicting feelings on his own, and would she not be better advised to stop playing the mother confessor? "Honesty" and "forgiveness" are being used to absolve the husband from facing up to his situation.

We usually think of honesty as providing clarity and improving relationships, and indeed it can. But the guise of honesty cannot. If honesty is motivated by one of these ulterior motives, then the relationship is not improved.

When is openness or honesty desirable, then? Is it when it will make me feel good? When it will get me what I want? When it will make my partner feel good? When it will help both of us to clarify and improve our relationship?

Think back over a good relationship and an unsatisfactory one that you have had. How much openness and honesty did you have in each? Did you use direct communication to improve the relationship, or did you use it to hurt or anger each other? Did you try to second-guess each other more in one relationship than the other? In which relationship were there more hidden intents or ulterior motives in communication? Does this tell you anything about how you want to use communication now?

Mixed Messages and the Double Entendre

Sometimes people intend a double message. One message is obvious and on the surface. Another message is indirect, obscure, perhaps nonverbal. The receivers are given a puzzle: should they respond to the surface message or the other one? Which is the real message?

The classic mixed message has been that of the woman who flirts with a man while having a conversation about art, politics, or some other nonsexual topic. He reads her eye, hand, and body movements and decides that she is inviting him to make a pass. If he does, she may be quite indignant. "What kind of girl do you think I am?" If he does not, the woman may be hurt or offended. "What a bore you are!"

This situation develops easily, since women have been expected to say no to a man even when they want to say yes. To get a yes message across, they have been limited to body language. The tradition is that women should not be forward. Therefore, men often ignore the verbal message and follow the nonverbal one. The unfortunate consequence of mass acceptance of this pattern is that women are left with hardly any way to say no and mean it. Some men then assume that all women mean yes when they say no, regardless of any message sent.

Is it harder for you to say yes or to say no? Are they both hard to say? Is it more difficult to ask for what you want or to ask what your partner wants? How hard is it for you to *hear* yes or no?

> Here is a series of statements about saying yes or no. Reflect on each one of them and decide to what extent the statement is characteristic of your own feeling and action.
>
> Place an X on the line after each statement to indicate where your attitudes tend to fall.
>
> 1. I won't go ahead with a sexual contact until I hear yes from my partner loud and clear.
>
> Completely un-   ————————————   Completely
> characteristic   1 2 3 4 5 6 7 8 9 10   characteristic
>
> 2. I enjoy resistance because I can have the fun of getting past the barriers my partner puts up.
>
> Completely un-   ————————————   Completely
> characteristic   1 2 3 4 5 6 7 8 9 10   characteristic

3. I don't like to ask for what I want, but I have all kinds of ways of getting my partner to give it to me anyway.

Completely un-characteristic   1   2   3   4   5   6   7   8   9   10   Completely characteristic

4. I sometimes enjoy leading my partner on and then saying no when they begin to act on my signals.

Completely un-characteristic   1   2   3   4   5   6   7   8   9   10   Completely characteristic

5. I don't like to ask for sex, and I don't like to hear yes or no. I like it to just happen naturally.

Completely un-characteristic   1   2   3   4   5   6   7   8   9   10   Completely characteristic

6. I like to have code words or actions with my partner, so we can let each other know what we want.

Completely un-characteristic   1   2   3   4   5   6   7   8   9   10   Completely characteristic

7. I find it hard to say no to my partner. I am afraid of being thought sexless.

Completely un-characteristic   1   2   3   4   5   6   7   8   9   10   Completely characteristic

8. I find it hard to say no to my partner about sex or anything else. I am afraid of an angry response.

Completely un-characteristic   1   2   3   4   5   6   7   8   9   10   Completely characteristic

9. I find it hard to say yes to any sexual overture. Somehow I feel it is safer to resist enough to keep the responsibility on the other person.

Completely un-characteristic   1   2   3   4   5   6   7   8   9   10   Completely characteristic

10. I find it hard to say yes to any sexual overture. I feel there is still something wrong with sex, even with my lover.

Completely un-characteristic   1   2   3   4   5   6   7   8   9   10   Completely characteristic

11. I like to keep the other person guessing. I don't like to come right out and say yes or no.

Completely un-characteristic _____ Completely characteristic

1   2   3   4   5   6   7   8   9   10

12. I like to be "taken by storm," have my partner toss all subtlety aside and just take me.

Completely un-characteristic _____ Completely characteristic

1   2   3   4   5   6   7   8   9   10

13. I like to take my partner "by storm" now and then, just rush in and grab what I want.

Completely un-characteristic _____ Completely characteristic

1   2   3   4   5   6   7   8   9   10

If you have an enduring sexual relationship, you and your partner may find it useful to compare the way you each answer the issues in this exercise.

Below is a scheme with which to interpret your responses. The numbers are those of the statements in the exercises. Circle any number where your response was 6 or higher.

It is hard for me to say yes: 9   10   11   12   13
It is hard for me to say no: 7   8   11   12   13
It is hard for me to ask for what I want: 1   3   5   6
It is hard for me to ask what my partner wants: 2   4   6
I don't like to hear yes or no: 2   5   6   13

Mixed messages can also cause a great deal of pain or confusion. If you are not clear about your own intents, they can hurt you as well as the other person. If you send an obscure message, you may not get the response you hope for. The other person may respond to a hidden intent when you desire a response to the surface message, or vice versa. Or if you use one issue to mask another, you are apt not to get either resolved successfully. Instead, you invite an attack.

Are there times in your sexual relationships when you feel misunderstood or when you regularly make the other person angry? Have you ever been accused of sending double messages?

If so, isolate a message you failed to get across, preferably one that has failed on more than one occasion. If you are alone, stand in front of a mirror and say your intended message out loud. Do your words sound clear to you? Now repeat the message nonverbally. Still standing in front of the mirror, use facial expressions and gestures to project your desired message. Then combine your verbal and nonverbal messages.

Does this feel right, or does it seem strange? Have you in the past tried to modify your verbal message with your nonverbal gestures? If you have, explore a new verbal and nonverbal message combination that is more consistent with your feelings.

If you cannot recall a mixed message to work on, but you and your partner occasionally do have misunderstandings, stop the next time one occurs and see if you can isolate the mixed message. Each of you give a nonverbal interpretation of what you *saw* the other say. Then give a verbal interpretation of what you *heard* the other say. Do these two messages agree? Are they what you each intended? Focus on clarifying the message, not on pinpointing who went wrong. This exercise is a lot of fun, so you may have to work hard to keep a straight face.

Developing awareness of the messages you are sending and taking responsibility for your half of the communication are two important steps toward improving any relationship. It may be reassuring to know that just because the message you intended went astray, you are not necessarily at fault. Your message could have been perfectly clear, but your partner did not hear it or misinterpreted it. Clear and faulty communications are each the responsibility of both persons. Trying to assign blame will hardly make things better and will more likely escalate confusions. Communication can be no better than the intentions of the two people who are speaking and listening.

Demanding the Impossible

Mixed intents and double messages are not the only source of communication difficulties. You may set out with the clearest of intentions, but other hazards may impede understanding. An especially nasty hazard is "demanding the impossible." A person may state a need or desire in such a way that it becomes impossible for the partner to fulfill. Here is how one couple got themselves in such a bind.

Bruce loved Lois, but he did wish that she would sometimes take the initiative in their lovemaking. She always seemed to follow his advances and mirror whatever mood he projected. If he was ecstatic, she was animated; if he was quiet, she was restrained. One night, when he was particularly fed up with her passivity, Bruce demanded that Lois be the initiator sometimes.

Lois took Bruce's wishes very much to heart and started trying to take the initiative. Being uncertain of herself and rather uncomfortable, however, she would end up saying to Bruce, "Am I doing all right? Is there anything else you want me to do?" He then felt as though he was still leading and that Lois was only doing what he "told" her to do. The more Bruce expressed his dissatisfaction with this, the more uptight Lois became about taking the initiative. The more he pressured her to take the initiative, the less he could feel she was taking it. He always had the nagging suspicion that she was only following "orders."

Consider the bind in each of the following messages: "Be more spontaneous, more abandoned, when we make love." "Be independent!" "Be more assertive!"

How can I order you to "be spontaneous"? If you adopt more uninhibited behavior, you will be doing just what I want. Or if you go out and find a lover or start a new job, how will I know whether you have done so because you are being independent or because I have told you to do so? Is your new assertiveness genuine, or are you passively following my demand for you to be so? In each case I have the difficulty of knowing whether you have really done what I hope for or not. Part of the difficulty is in the paradoxical character of the wish itself. That is a fact that cannot be changed. However, part of the difficulty is in the demanding mentality. If such a desire is expressed honestly and gently, it can often be fulfilled by the cooperative experiments of the partners. As a unilateral demand of one partner, it provides simply another source of contention.

Key Words and Mismatched Meanings

Misinterpretation of the other person's intent is another common source of communication failure. People misread each other's behavior because of different understandings of a key value. In this book we have occasionally asked you to define for yourself a key value word, such as *love, fidelity,* or *commitment.* We learn the meaning of these emotion-laden words from our upbringing and the situations in which we have experienced their use. Thus, when two persons with widely differing experiences start relating, there are bound to be some confusions over the behaviors that are expected to go with these words.

Joan thinks that if Mac really loved her, he would bring her flowers occasionally and be more demonstrative in public. After all, this is what her father did for her mother, and he certainly loved her. Since Mac does not do this, she accuses him of not loving her. Mac, however, feels that one shows one's love by providing a good home and financial security for one's loved one, and he does this very well. Thus, he feels unjustly accused by Joan and thinks she is being ungrateful. They have never discussed what each means by *love*—they have only flung the word back and forth at each other in angry and tearful conversations.

Sit back and listen to some old arguments that you had with a sexual partner. Are there any words like *love, commitment,* or *faithfulness* that kept popping up in these conversations? Are you sure that you knew what your partner meant by this word? Are you sure that your partner knew what you meant when you used it? Did you understand the past that gave the word its meaning for each of you?

Have you exchanged vows with someone? If so, are you certain you have similar understandings of the words you said?

If you have used the vows of a religious service, you might go over the vows together. What do such words as *love, honor, cherish,* and *forsaking all others* mean to each of you? Do you interpret these words and phrases similarly or differently? Can you resolve the differences, or are they unimportant?

Sexual behaviors are particularly apt to be misinterpreted. What is meaningless playful flirtation for one person may be interpreted as seduction by another. What a man considers to be desirable masculine behavior may be seen as overly aggressive, sexist boorishness by the woman he is trying to impress. What a woman considers to be enticing feminine behavior may be seen as overly dependent, weak, clinging behavior by the man she is trying to attract. If signals are misinterpreted at the outset, and there is no direct communication to straighten them out, then a well-meaning attempt at relationship is bound to falter.

Failure to communicate directly, of course, can also occur in ongoing relationships. Misinterpretation and second-guessing can each reinforce the other to produce very volatile situations. For example, here is a situation we were asked to conciliate.

Liz had been having an affair with Peter for the past two months. She occasionally thought she would like to tell her husband, Art, about it, but each time she lost her nerve. Art got so upset when she flirted playfully with men at parties that she felt that he could not possibly handle knowing about her affair. Jealousy would consume him.

Instead, after a party, Liz teased Art about a woman who had flirted with him and suggested that he might like to have an affair. She thought that by using this indirect approach she might get Art to understand how harmless a little sexual fling is. Art, however, reacted angrily, "How could you possibly think that all I want with a woman is to screw?" At this point communication broke off. Art remained insulted that Liz would even suggest that he behave in such a fashion, and Liz became more convinced than ever that Art would explode if she told him about Peter.

The pressures of guilt and secrecy, however, continued to build in Liz, so finally she went so far as to tell Art that she had a good male friend whom she would like him to meet. This was by no means complete disclosure, but to her surprise, Art responded calmly and said he would like that.

From our vantage point, Liz and Art have a conflict in value systems. They attach different meanings to the sexual act. Art can approve more of Liz having a close male friend than he can of her flirtations—but of course Liz used the term *close friend* because she could not bear to say *lover*. Therefore, this couple still has a long way to go if they are to clear up their misunderstandings. They must not only have a better grasp of each other's values, but they also need to find a way to live comfortably with their differing value systems.

R. D. Laing has suggested that much of this kind of guessing, or "metacommunication," as he calls it, takes place when there is mistrust in a relationship. The more mistrust there is, the more two people are likely to stop talking directly and try to interpret or outguess each other instead.[3] Yet, by hiding things and acting out of their guesses about each other's behavior, they are not giving themselves the chance to reduce their mistrust. Liz and Art might still have problems if they level with each other, but as long as they are misinterpreting what each believes, their chances of sorting things out are slim indeed.

Matched Meanings

Do you ever feel that you and your partner are misunderstanding each other's preferences in sexual activity? Are there gaps in your communication about lovemaking?

A. Answer the following questions about your partner. After you answer each, consider whether your answer is based on facts you believe to be true because you have openly discussed the matter or is based on guesses that you have made from indirect messages. Invite your partner to do this exercise, too. Afterward, check out the accuracy of your responses with each other.

1. Where does your partner like to have sexual activity? In bed only or in a variety of locations? List likely places.

2. When does your partner like to have sexual activity? Nighttime only? Morning only? Any time? Specify.

3. What positions does your partner like? You on top? Your partner on top? Side by side? Sitting? Standing? Rear entry? Others?

4. What varieties of body contact give your partner erotic pleasure? (If you are unsure of this, go back to the chart where you mapped your erotic contact preferences. Did you and your partner exchange charts at the time? If not, try to guess each other's preferences now and exchange charts.)

5. Does your partner have any strong dislikes in the above areas? If so, list them.

B. Below are some questions that explore the manner in which you and your partner like sexual activity—a sexual activity profile. The answers to the questions usually involve matters of degree, and so there is a continuum after each question. Put an S at the point that represents how you respond to the question for your*self*. Put a P at the point that you think marks your *partner's* position. If neither you nor your partner has any preferences on a given matter, then ignore that question. Do not let your partner see your responses until he or she has also had the opportunity to do the profile.

1. How much privacy do you need to enjoy sexual activity?

Absolutely certain privacy   High risk of discovery

| 1 | 2 | 3 | 4 | 5 | 6 | 7 | 8 | 9 | 10 |

2. How frequently do you want sex?

Less than once a month   More than once a day

| 1 | 2 | 3 | 4 | 5 | 6 | 7 | 8 | 9 | 10 |

3. How do you feel about wearing clothes while having sex?

Want to be fully clothed									Want to be fully nude
1	2	3	4	5	6	7	8	9	10

4. Do you like making love in the light or in the dark?

Always in the dark									Always with light
1	2	3	4	5	6	7	8	9	10

5. How much erotic touching or foreplay before orgasm do you like?

Next to none									Extensive
1	2	3	4	5	6	7	8	9	10

6. Do you enjoy making love in a certain manner?

Yes—like established routines or rituals									No—like spontaneity and variety
1	2	3	4	5	6	7	8	9	10

7. Do you like close, overall body contact while having sex?

No—genital contact only									Yes—extensive body contact
1	2	3	4	5	6	7	8	9	10

8. Do you like moans or noises during lovemaking?

No—never									Yes—lots
1	2	3	4	5	6	7	8	9	10

9. Do you like to set the mood with music?

Never									Always
1	2	3	4	5	6	7	8	9	10

10. Who do you want to initiate sexual activity?

Always myself									Always my partner
1	2	3	4	5	6	7	8	9	10

11. Do you like conversation during lovemaking?

No—never   Yes—lots

1	2	3	4	5	6	7	8	9	10

12. Do you enjoy fantasies while having sex?

No—never   Yes—always

1	2	3	4	5	6	7	8	9	10

13. Do you like lovemaking to be slow or fast?

Slow   Fast

1	2	3	4	5	6	7	8	9	10

14. Do you like lovemaking to be rough or gentle?

Rough   Gentle

1	2	3	4	5	6	7	8	9	10

When both of you have completed these questions, compare your P markings with your partner's S markings, and vice versa. Do you have any significant misperceptions or misinterpretations of each other's responses to any question?

Then, connect your S markings from question to question down the page. Put your partner's S markings on the same page with yours and connect his or her markings. Use a different color pen or pencil so that it will be clear whose profile is which. Are your profiles similar or very different? Or do you perhaps differ on one or two items only?

Comparing S and P markings may in itself resolve troublesome issues arising from gaps or misinterpretations in communication. On the other hand, these profiles may only clarify areas of conflict. These may be conflicts over specific issues, such as lights on or lights off, or more fundamental differences in style. For example, if one person's profile is consistently much farther to the right on questions 1 to 9 than the other's, this may indicate a basic conflict in the amount of risk, expressiveness, or variety that each wants in sexual activity.

The important thing here is not whether you are in total agreement but whether you are developing a style of communication that will enable you to deal with unresolved issues between you. Frequently people are afraid to face murky issues directly for fear of the conflict that might arise. Yet often this murkiness itself leads to conflict and unhappiness. It is difficult to resolve an issue that is not being talked about. Direct, nonblaming communication offers the possibility, although not the certainty, of a more creative solution to the divisive issues of sexual differences.

Clues to Clearer Communication

We have seen so many hazards, perhaps you are now wondering if good communication is possible at all. Actually each of the pitfalls contains a clue to clearer communication. You may find a summary of these hints useful if communication is a value you want to emphasize.

Sending Messages

1. *Speak for yourself.* Don't generalize about the nature of the world or interpret what other people think or feel. Take direct responsibility for your own thoughts and feelings. Dick says to Jane, "People get a lot out of sex if they really let themselves go." Jane says to Dick, "But you grow up learning it's bad to be too sexy." Dick and Jane are being vague and sneaky, making statements about life in general. Dick could have said, "I would like us to try some really way-out sex." Jane could have said, "I don't know if I can; I've listened so long to the message that 'nice girls don't do that.' " Here they are each speaking for themselves, taking responsibility for their own feelings. Be on the lookout in your own speech for phrases like these: "One doesn't enjoy . . ."; "You feel used when . . ."; "They take advantage of . . ."; "We don't want. . . ." Be suspicious of every pronoun except *I*.

There are two sides to this coin. You speak for yourself and you let others speak for themselves. Gestalt therapy has long emphasized this, rejecting every so-called interpretation. You do not know how your partner feels, and you therefore cannot *interpret* to them or for them how it is with them. Masters and Johnson express this in their method of treatment by training sexual partners to use "*I* language." No woman knows what a male erection feels like, and no man knows what a female orgasm is like. Not only are men and women different, but individuals are different. If communication is to improve, each person must learn to say *I*: "I feel . . ."; "*I* like . . ."; "*I* want. . . ." Fortunately it is a very simple thing to learn, and it makes all the difference in the world.

2. *Make direct statements.* If you are clear about what you want to communicate, it works best if you simply state it flat out. We make indirect

statements often out of cowardice. If I ask to make love, you may say no and I will feel foolish. So I hint.

When Charles and Mary first had intercourse, she failed to have an orgasm, but not wanting to embarrass herself or him, she pretended that she did. A little later she began to hint that things were not quite right for her, but Charles did not get the message, so she went on pretending. This little charade seemed harmless enough at the outset, but ten years later it was still going on, wreaking sexual havoc. Their whole lives might have been different if on the very first occasion Mary had said something like this: "Charles, I really feel foolish saying this, but I did not have an orgasm. I like you a lot, and I feel we can really enjoy sex together. But I may need to learn to relax with you." Then if Mary had some notion of what she needed, such as a different position, she could ask for that. It is a lot easier to begin with direct communication than to switch after years of indirect hints.

3. *Match words and gestures.* If your body language and your words agree, a clearer message will get across. If they don't, you may be confused yourself about what you want to say. You may be sending two messages. Perhaps there will be times when you choose to communicate on two different levels. However, when you want to communicate a specific message clearly, then let your eyes and hands say the same thing your mouth is saying. You may even learn something about what you really want your mouth to say by becoming aware of what your body is doing.

4. *Make a clear value choice about how honest and open you wish to be.* You remain a fuzzy communicator as long as you are unclear about how much you want to communicate. Not only do I choose how open to be in every situation, I also make some long-range choices that determine my style of communication. Others learn the meaning of my signs, signals, and words. If I am a teller of tall tales one day and take on the guise of absolute frankness another, those near me are left confused about how to interpret my words and actions. If I want to be a clear communicator, I must choose a more or less habitual style of communication.

Receiving Messages

1. *Don't guess; check it out.* The magic of good communication is asking, not mind reading. Of course, you don't have to stop in the middle of making torrid love and say, "Does this feel good?" Nevertheless, unless your partner's words and body have told you unambiguously what you need or want to know, pick an appropriate time and place and have a conversation to check out the accuracy of what you think you see or hear.

2. *Listen to body language as well as words.* Neither you nor your partner is a perfectly clear communicator. Therefore, you need to listen to each other's words and gestures. Gestures have a certain priority over language. When word and gesture do not agree, gesture usually reflects more accurately what the person is actually feeling. Body language is not so easily censored, and body language may add color and subtlety to a verbal message already clear and straight. Do not assume as a result of your sensitivity to body language that you know better than others do what they think or feel. Instead, check it out.

3. *Mirror back to your partner what you think you hear.* Psychologist Carl Rogers made a great discovery when he found that reflecting back to a person what you think you hear from that person produces miraculous results. In this way, you check out the accuracy of your listening and you help your partner to further explore his or her feelings. It is a wonderful experience to feel that you have really been heard, that someone understands what you are saying. This is a simple device, but it takes some practice. You do not parrot back the words said, but you put in your own words what you have heard.

4. *Make a clear value choice about what kind of listener you will be.* As with openness, listening is a value choice. It would be absurd to assume that the more you listen, the better. You would cease to function entirely if all you did was listen. No, you choose how much to listen. You listen different amounts in different situations, and further, you choose a style of listening that becomes characteristic of you. You do not want to be a sponge, soaking up everything around you, nor a rock, taking nothing in. Between these extremes you make your choices. If you seem to listen with some consistency, then your partner and others can depend upon your listening and trust your insights.

13

Battles below the Belt

A blow to the genitals is a low blow. Conflict about sex is painful indeed. Yet you choose a fighting style as a part of your sexual style, since conflict over sex is as common as sex itself. Let's sketch some quick cartoons of three kinds of fighters.

First, there are the heavyweights. They are willing to fight—win, lose, or draw. They never run, they don't beat up on littler folks, and they never hit below the belt—not on purpose, at least. The fight is short; three rounds is enough. When the bell rings, they embrace their opponent with affection and respect.

Then there are the lightweights. They depend more on speed than on power, and they can take on a heavier fighter by staying out of reach. They dart in for a jab and are gone again before another blow can be struck. They don't always win, but they never lose. They leave. Some lightweights leave before a fight really gets under way. If it looks like the fight may break out again, they may decide not to come back at all. Actually, they are better at track than at boxing.

Finally, there are the fight-hall professionals. They may be good fighters or poor, heavyweight or lightweight, but they seem to enjoy fighting and they do it frequently. Fighting is a way of life with them. Nothing ever gets decided, so they just keep on fighting. There is some pay in it, not a lot, but they can always have a fight when television gets boring.

In this chapter we will give primary attention to the heavyweights. In our experience, sexual partners choose the other two styles only when the first one has failed. Of course, sexual partners can fall into using all sorts of devices to avoid or minimize conflict, just as they can become habituated to fighting. However, in either case this happens unintentionally. To be values, these styles must be chosen in the awareness of other available options. After having tried to resolve issues in conflict, a couple decide to end an unviable sexual relationship. That is a conscious choice and a value. Similarly, accepting an unresolved sexual conflict can be a choice made for the sake of other values present in the relationship. Thus, we will note the lightweight and professional styles of fighting only as the methods of last resort when a stalemate occurs.

Consider the following situations. Which response would be closest to your own in each case?

1. You are a woman who enjoys having several orgasms in an hour of lovemaking. You have been living with a man who has his orgasm very quickly and withdraws. He seems to think your sex life is great, but you have been increasingly frustrated and unsatisfied. You have not talked about your frustration, but you can feel the pressure building to do so. In fact, you realized last night that if you don't talk soon, you are likely to curse his quickness in bed one of these times. What will you say or do?

   a. Wait for your explosion to occur and then make the best of it.
   b. Get out of the relationship before the explosion occurs and look for a new sexual partner who is not so quick.
   c. Tell him that the sexual pattern the two of you have developed is not fulfilling your sexual needs and suggest you explore together ways that it might be made more fulfilling.
   d. Tell him that he is no good in bed and should see a sex therapist.
   e. Tell him that he needs to slow down and you would like to help him do that so that he can become more satisfying to you—you are sure he can do it if he tries.

2. You are the man with the "quickness problem" in the preceding situation. Your partner is multiorgasmic, and she has just made response *e.* That is, she has told you that for her to get sexual satisfaction, you need to slow down. She is willing to help you in any way she can—she has heard that there are books that explain how to cure your problem. What's more, she is sure you can do it if you just try. What will you say or do?

   a. Tell her if she doesn't like the way you do it, she can get out.
   b. Tell her if she wants sexual satisfaction, then she had better learn to speed up. Real men don't mess around.

c. Tell her you have done some reading on the subject yourself and know that if you "try," you will only make things worse. Instead, could you explore together ways of improving sex for both of you?

d. Gratefully accept her offer, and ask where you can get such a book. You know your current sexual performance is inadequate. You are willing to do everything in your power to please her.

e. Confess to her that you have always had this problem and that other women have tried to help you but nothing seems to work. You guess you are just no good in bed and are sincerely sorry for that.

f. Laugh at your darling's Florence Nightingale earnestness and quickly change the subject.

One response in each case offers the best possibility for creative conflict. That is response c. It may have been fairly easy for you to pick out the constructive response. Yet it may be much more difficult for you actually to make that response in both situations. Many people can readily make that response in the first situation but not in the second. If one's sexual ability has already been called into question, then the tendency is to return the attack or to try to shrug off the sexual slur. It takes a very secure person to ignore ego-deflating comments and to respond with constructive suggestions.

3. Now suppose that our multiorgasmic woman had made a type c response. That is, she said something like, "You know, I've been feeling increasingly frustrated lately and probably should have said something sooner to let you know how it is with me. I really need more foreplay or some fondling of my genitals after intercourse in order to relieve the tension built up while you are having your orgasm and to get my own enjoyment. Do you think we could change our lovemaking pattern a bit to deal with my sexual needs?" What might your response be as the man? Scribble a brief response.

It is probably easier to respond constructively in this situation than it was in situation 2. Once conflicts begin to get out of hand it is very difficult to correct the damage already done and to achieve a useful dialogue. Becoming more aware of the signs of harmful or pointless conflict and the ways to state grievances constructively are important first steps to conflict management. As we look at ways of dealing with conflict, keep in mind your responses to these opening situations. You may be able to isolate some patterns in your own relationships that make potentially useful conflict destructive instead.

Sexual Short Circuits

Many couples never come to grips with their basic problems because the discussion short-circuits before it can begin. This happens in a variety of ways. One of the most common is by blaming, attacking, or otherwise finding fault with the other person. "It's not my problem; it's yours." This can be done very blatantly, as when our woman says, "You're no good in bed; you should see a sex therapist." Or it can be done more subtly, as in the example where she offers to help her partner sort out his problem.

Either of these opening gambits is like waving a red flag. Defenses are readied, and an attack or abrupt withdrawal follows. Thus, our man might have told his partner either to get out or to speed up: "Real men don't mess around." In other words, "The problem is yours, not mine." If he did this, the couple could go on tossing the blame ball back and forth indefinitely. They may release a lot of anger, but the real issue is not dealt with.

Another way to short-circuit the discussion is to become very apologetic. Thus, the man might tell the woman that he knows he is a lousy lover, that he has always had this "problem," and that nothing he has ever tried worked. Such a person is basically saying, "I'm so terrible, you can't possibly expect me to change." By cataloguing his own inadequacies, he offers further "proof" that he cannot be any different from what he is. With luck, his partner will feel so guilty about ever having brought the subject up, she will not mention it again.

Both of these methods, of course, can lead to very nasty scenes. Moreover, destroying your own self-esteem is as unpleasant as having someone else destroy it for you. However, there are still other methods of avoidance to choose from. One can leave the relationship at the first sight of a major conflict, hit and run, or just run. Or one may do this issue by issue, subtly deflecting the topic of conversation wherever a disagreement looms. Thus, our man may make some joke about his "little Florence Nightingale, who is always willing to help anyone in distress"; thank her charmingly for her offer; and smoothly change the subject. Issues can be left unresolved for years this way.

Think of your three most recent conflicts with your sexual partner or your three most recent near conflicts. Did you or your partner end up using one of these ploys? Did you resolve the issue you originally wanted to or not?

If discussion of your basic issue was short-circuited, replay the conversation that took place in your mind. Could you have said something that would have reduced the attacks on each other's self-esteem or redirected the conversation to the basic issue? Mentally rehearse a new style of response right now.

Facing Conflict

If you have thought of a better way in which you could have handled a recent conflict, you probably will have a chance to try it out. Issues that are avoided or left unresolved have a tendency to pop up again. If the basic disagreement has not been handled, then tensions are likely to form again around the same issue.

You can wait until these tensions once again become so great that you feel an explosion about to take place. Alternatively, you can bring up the subject before this point is reached. Usually it is easier to state your feelings and needs constructively when you are just somewhat tense about an issue than when you have reached a blind fury. How many times have you let anger build up to uncontrollable levels and then said things that were stupid and regrettable?

Facing into conflict involves following some rather commonsensical procedures. To begin with, it involves avoiding the hazards of communication that we explored in the last chapter. Mixed messages and ulterior motives are particularly apt to turn a good fight into a bad one. Most of the short circuits we have just looked at involve switching the message, either deliberately or unconsciously, from the subject at hand to "Look how terrible you are/I am."

Then, too, misinterpretation of each other's messages causes much unproductive conflict. We suggested checking out the meanings of key words in the last chapter. However, if you feel that your messages still are not coming across clearly to each other, the following exercise may be helpful. It is based on the method of listening developed by Carl Rogers and can be used in many different situations.

Whenever your fighting is going out of control, stop. Begin the conversation again. Let one of you state a grievance. Before responding to this statement, the other person must repeat it in *his or her own words*. When the first person is satisfied that this rephrasing accurately reflects the original statement, then the second person has earned the right to make his or her own response. The first person must then go through the same procedure—earning the right to reply only when he or she has accurately reflected the second person's response. This process is continued as long as it is useful.

This procedure is guaranteed to slow down an argument, but it is remarkable in improving understanding. Moreover, it helps to develop skill at listening to each other—one of the most important communicative skills.

Sometimes the "objective" data on which a fight is based need to be checked out. Partners occasionally place sexual demands on each other that are impossible or improbable. If a woman tells a man to try harder, he is apt to do worse rather than better. For a man to tell a woman to speed up would be equally pointless. Technical information may be useful in such cases of conflict. In any conflict it can be useful to check out the feeling response or the grievance with specific behavioral data. If a man would like to make love more often, he could say, "Why don't you ever want to make love? Don't you love me anymore?" Or he could say, "You know, we haven't made love since last Tuesday, and I am feeling bad about it. Somehow I've gotten the signals that you didn't want to when I did. Is that so, or have I misread you?" The first opening gambit will cause his partner to defend herself. The second gives some clear issues for her to respond to and is far less accusatory.

Collecting and exchanging information, however, can be carried to extremes and become an avoidance device itself. There are "human computer" types who constantly seem to be collecting and analyzing data, never venturing an opinion or feeling of their own. Thus, this man's partner could respond by saying, "Oh, that's funny, I'm sure we made love on Wednesday. Remember, we had just watched that movie on television." A full-scale argument might then ensue about whether it was Tuesday or Wednesday. The issue switches to who has the best memory. This has nothing to do with the man's feeling of rejection but indeed might increase it. Or his partner could ask him to recite in detail every facial expression and gesture that led him to feel she did not want to make love, sagely murmuring, "Mmm. Oh, how interesting." Again much data might emerge, but only about him, and the central issue would have been avoided.

When you and your partner fight, how do you use data?

Never look at the data								Drown the argument in facts	
1	2	3	4	5	6	7	8	9	10

When a sexual conflict starts, it is worth wondering, "Is this the subject we really want to fight about?" This may sound like a strange question, but many couples let arguments about finances, job obligations, or raising children spill over into the sexual arena, or vice versa. One couple complained to us about their sexual conflict, in which the wife did not like to have her breasts or genitals fondled. Gradually it became clear that the woman was very angry at her husband because she did not feel he shared enough of the childrearing and household responsibilities. (They both had jobs.) Once she pinpointed her real anger, she also realized she had been using sex as a way to get back at her husband. She then made a conscious decision to fight out her domestic frustrations in the kitchen and not in bed. They soon reported improvement in their sex life. It remains to be seen how things turn out in the kitchen.

This spill-over effect may be why many couples report having much better sex right after they have had a good fight that has cleared the air. Have you ever had that experience? Negative feelings in one area hold back good feelings in other areas of a relationship. When conflict is resolved in one area, it also releases good feelings in others.

One of the common sources of sexual conflict is jealousy. We all know that jealousy is "bad." One partner tries to limit the behavior of the other through threats, accusations, or demands for change. Yet the bases of jealousy are natural and even useful as a form of self-protection. Jealousy says, "I am hurting, and I fear greater hurt and loss. Help me to feel better and more secure."

Consider these two situations:

1. Dick and Jane have been living together for five years. Neither has ever altered the dinner hour without asking permission in advance. Most evenings they cuddle up together to read or watch television. They have had regular, enjoyable sex. For the last three weeks, however, Dick has stopped coming home punctually and has not even informed Jane beforehand. Two nights ago, Dick did not come home at all. When Dick rolls in at 3 A.M. tonight, Jane is still awake and explodes, "Where have you been? What on earth have you been doing? Don't I count anymore?"

2. Jack and Jill have been living together for five years. Neither has ever altered the dinner hour without advance arrangements. Most evenings they cuddle up together in front of television or read. They have had regular, enjoyable sex together. For the last three weeks, however, Jill has become very inquisitive about Jack's whereabouts at

all times. She has been calling him up at work "to check in." She has refused to attend a play with a friend because Jack could not go along. Two nights ago when he got home twenty minutes late, she grilled him for a half-hour about what had happened. Tonight when he comes in a few minutes late again, she explodes, "Where have you been? What one earth have you been doing? Don't I count anymore?"

Are both women making a jealous response? What for you is the difference between reasonable self-protective behavior and unreasonable jealousy?

Both women say the same thing, but no doubt you thought Jane was much more justified than Jill in her response. Suppose Jane has said something like, "Oh, you're late again. Did you have a good time, dear? I do like to see you enjoying yourself." Such a response would have seemed unnatural or uncaring, would it not? Either Jane did not want Dick enough to care if he left her, or she enjoys getting hurt. For Jill, however, such a response would surely have been more appropriate to the circumstances than the one she actually made.

What makes the difference in the two cases? Clearly, in Jill's case there is little or no evidence that Jack is behaving any differently than he always has done. Her newly developed insecurity must have other sources. The changes seem to be in her: she has developed some strange new anxiety. In Jane's case, there does seem to be a real basis. Dick's behavior has changed. Her response may not have been the ideal way to handle the situation, but certainly her fear was a natural reaction to Dick's changes.

To make sure that you and your partner are not misunderstanding or imagining things about each other's sexual style, you might like to use the following strategy. You can sort out the issues that are causing unnecessary conflict from issues that the two of you really do want to resolve. If you do not now have an ongoing relationship with someone, you may still wish to do this with a sexual partner to check out how well you are "reading" each other.

Put each of the following questions on a separate piece of paper. Have your partner do the same. Then list as many responses as you can to each question. Do not compare answers until you are finished.

1. What are the important features of my sexual style?

2. What are the important features of my partner's sexual style?

3. What does my partner think are the important features of my sexual style?

When you have both finished, compare your responses to question 1. This will show how nearly you actually agree on a choice of a sexual style. Next compare your question 2 responses with your partner's question 1 responses. These will show how well you "know" your partner. Have you misunderstood any essential features of your partner's sexual preferences? Reverse the process and have your partner compare his or her 2 responses with your 1 responses. How well does he or she "know" you? Finally, compare your responses to question 3 with your partner's responses to question 2, and vice versa. This will show how misunderstood either of you feels.

If you go through these comparisons carefully, you may find a number of misunderstandings suddenly cleared up. You may find a number of issues on which you thought you disagreed, but in fact you do not. You may also discover an issue on which you currently conflict that a brief discussion will resolve. We have found that for many people, just getting the issues down in writing helps them see a way to clear them up. On the other hand, you may be brought face to face with some important disagreements in your relationship. These are the ones over which conflict can be most fruitful. Having some good, fair fights over them may produce a much more creative and satisfying relationship.

This does not mean that if you isolate your basic conflict(s), change and harmony will automatically occur. Some conflicts are the result of differing values that are deeply ingrained. For example, most women have been taught to be a helpmate in a total marriage. Most men, however, have learned to put a job before a marriage. It may not be realistic to expect yourself or your partner to change long-established patterns overnight. However, if you both agree on the need to find a creative solution to your conflict, if you are both willing to make adjustments, then the old ruts can lead to a new way.

Answering the three questions and comparing responses is a good problem finder. It is also a good empathy builder. Empathy, the ability to understand your partner's feelings, is a crucial asset in solving conflict. It is so easy to think only of *my* rights, *my* needs, *my* hurts, and so on. Yet argument is not fruitful while each person is busy protecting or extending his or her own self-interests. It takes two to have a fight, and usually, perhaps always, there are some rights and some wrongs on both sides. Empathy is the bridge that links your side with my side of the issue. I can cross over and see the issue from your side. It may give one of us the fresh insight that suggests a creative approach that never occurred to either of us before.

If you and your partner desire somewhat different sexual styles, try an exercise in empathy:

1. Imagine giving your partner permission to lead the sexual style he or she desires. Would you need to change for your partner to succeed, or could you retain your present style? What changes would be likely to occur in your relationship? What is the worst that could happen? What is the best?

Now imagine the reverse: your partner gives you permission to pursue the sexual style of your choice. Would your partner need or not need to change for you to succeed? What changes would be likely to occur in your relationship? What is the worst that could happen? What is the best?

Is the best much better in one of these two cases, or the worst much worse? Can you understand the feelings of your partner any better?

2. List all the advantages for yourself in pursuing the sexual style you desire. List all the advantages for your partner and/or your relationship. List all the disadvantages for your partner and/or your relationship.

Now do the same for your partner's preferred sexual style: list all the advantages for your partner in pursuing the sexual style he or she desires. List all the advantages for yourself and/or your relationship. List all the disadvantages for yourself and/or your relationship.

3. When you have finished considering both your and your partner's preferred sexual styles, pause for a moment to consider the possibility of some compromise between your two styles. Imagine a sexual style somewhere in between your two preferred styles that minimizes the disadvantages you see in each other's styles and capitalizes on the advantages. Can you do this?

After your partner has done this exercise, try to create together a vision of a mutually satisfying sexual style. Are you now more sensitive to each other's hurts, needs, and desires?

Stalemate

"I've tried everything, but this old tension just sits here like a pain in the pit of my stomach." Sadly, neither the procedures suggested here nor one's own best efforts will resolve tragic conflicts for everyone. So the question arises, What should my partner and I do if we seem to be faced with an unresolvable conflict?

One option is to try to ignore the conflict and carry on. Some people can compartmentalize and set limits on their conflict fairly successfully. They agree to differ in certain respects. For example, one partner who wants to be exclusive may turn a blind eye to the other person's sexual escapades, demanding only discretion and some restraint. Some people, however, cannot do this. If you have a basic sexual conflict, can you set limits to it? Would you want to pursue this option?

Another option is to keep on arguing. There are couples who seem to make conflict a way of life. They expect conflict to be a natural and constant part of their relationship. They are not necessarily unhappy or miserable. Perhaps they derive some satisfaction from fighting. Do you do this? Does this option work for you?

A third option is to terminate the relationship. Certainly there are destructive relationships in which such drastic action is necessary. One person can constantly try to protect his or her ego by blaming the other. One partner may be so insecure and jealous that he or she uncontrollably demands a minute-by-minute account of the other's actions or whereabouts. One partner may abuse the other physically or psychologically. In some cases the only healthy alternative may be to get out.

Here is such a case: Maureen and Tom got married with an understanding that both would be free to have sex with anyone they wished. As it turned out, for several years only Tom indulged in this privilege. He sometimes brought sexual partners to their small apartment and was completely unconcerned whether Maureen was there or not. In fact, on several occasions Tom called Maureen into the bedroom where he and his friend were cuddling after intercourse, to ask for a drink or breakfast. At length, Maureen told Tom she was unhappy with all this, but he dismissed her complaints as old-fashioned jealousy. Half believing him, she began an affair of her own, but when she told Tom, he attacked her physically and threatened to kill her. The marriage was quickly ended. Tom was unable to enter into mutuality with Maureen, and she was unable to protect her interests in the relationship.

There are, however, people who end any relationship at the first sign of conflict. People who are unmarried may do this more easily, but some follow this course of action in marriage as well. Essentially, they seek to avoid conflict by getting out. What do you think? When, if ever, is termination an appropriate option? How bad would things have to get for you before you would consider termination?

In all the discussion of sex and sexual conflicts in this book, it can be easy to let these issues assume an importance out of all proportion to the rest of your relationship. Below is a balance scale in which to judge whether this has in fact happened. If you and your partner have a serious sexual difficulty that has made you consider ending the relationship, list it on the left side of the balance. On the right side, list the positive aspects of your relationship. Do they more than balance the negative sexual factor? Are there any other negative factors you would like to consider in the overall estimation of your relationship? Any more positive things? If so, list them.

Negative factors that might make me consider ending this relationship	Positive factors that make this relationship worth continuing

Which side seems to carry more weight?

If this exercise leaves you uncertain about the quality or worth of the relationship you are currently in, you may want to consider yet another option: seeking outside expert help for your problem. What help you seek would depend on the nature of your conflict. You could go to a couples communication course if talking about issues in conflict seems to be your greatest difficulty. On the other hand, a sex therapist would probably be most useful if one or the other of you suffers a specific sexual dysfunction, such as not being orgasmic or ejaculating sooner than desired. There is a wide range of counselors and therapists who will deal with more general problems of sexual relationship, as well as religious advisers who will help sort out sexual problems focused on moral issues. Some suggestions of where to look for outside help are given in the Bibliography.

Not all chess games end in stalemate, and neither do most sexual relationships. Thoughts of termination or therapy may be far from your mind. Instead, you may feel that fruitful change or growth is already within your reach. You just need the time and some encouragement to deploy your own resources. If so, then the next chapter will help you on your way.

14

Charting Change

Change can be scary, the specter of the unknown quite frightening. To change your sexual style might result in a major upheaval in your life. Besides, change is hard work. Long-accustomed habit is not lightly left behind, nor are new ways of thought and action a simple matter of decision. Changing your sexual style is not a free ride on a giant slide, careening you happily into a new sex pool with a giggling splash.

"So who says I want to change, anyway? Looking at this parade of sexual styles has convinced me more than ever that the way I am is right for me." We often hear words like these from people who have completed this exploration of sexual values. Do you feel this way now? If, indeed, your style satisfies your needs and fundamentally supports the values you wish to affirm, our purpose has been amply fulfilled. You are now pleased with yourself and your sexual style. You recognize your way of being sexual as a conscientious choice and not an accident of physiology or birth. It is a good feeling, isn't it, to realize that your choices are good ones?

However, this is what we hear more often: "It's time for a change! Looking at all these possibilities has made me realize there are some things I really do want to deal with." Do you feel this way now? There may be only a few things you wish to change, a detail here or there. Or you may be thinking about a sharp right or left turn. If change is scary and takes effort, it can also be a marvelous adventure. You don't have to thrash out blindly into an unknown jungle. There have been others who have gone before you.

Besides, change does not demand that you grit your teeth for hours on end. It is more like the serious play of children, undertaken with intensity and joy. The achievement is not a product painstakingly fashioned. Something much more profound takes place quietly within. The effort required is more a willingness to "let go" and "let happen" than any titanic thrusting of energy. Perhaps the image of a giant slide is not completely wrong. You choose your slide with care. You search for one that has the speed and inclination you want, looking out for any loose metal or splintering wood, inspecting the spot where you will land. You don't want to bounce onto concrete at full speed. Having observed it thoughtfully, you climb briskly to the top and let yourself go, knowing you cannot enjoy the ride so long as you nervously hold onto the sides.

Tough Questions

Let's look over the slide you are considering. Here are three tough questions to ask yourself:

Do I have the facts? By now you have read more than once that facts do not make your choices for you. But you do need any available important and relevant facts in order to make wise choices. There is no virtue in ignorance. What kind of facts do you look for?

First, you look for facts about sexual function. You may need more understanding of the way sexual organs respond in order to make your decision. One woman felt a failure in pleasuring her partner when his erection flagged after an hour of sex play. She needed to know a very simple fact: the erection of the penis naturally waxes and wanes. No new technique of stimulation will change that. Of course, the situation might have been worse. She might have thought there was something wrong with her partner when his erection departed. Had she communicated that to an insecure male, his erection might have taken permanent flight.

Technique, however, is a second kind of information that is of some importance to sexual style. For example, trying to be more sexually expressive might lead a male to rub more vigorously and persistently on the clitoris of his partner. If he does, she will be better off if a further ignorance leads him to seek the clitoris where it is not to be found. If you wish to be more expressive sexually, you can look for more information on sexual technique, on massage, "hot tubs," or sensual pleasuring. Let other people's imagination inspire your own. Books, films, and magazines may help you.

Finally, you look for facts about the specific sexual style you are considering. Here we use the word *facts* loosely, since what you will find is more expert opinion than scientific fact. Styles involve values, and science is not often expert when it comes to values. You may then need to seek your information from books, articles, or persons who advocate the style you are thinking about. They can tell you how wonderful it all is! If the advocates cannot make the style sound attractive, then you are probably not interested anyway. If, however, the style retains or increases its appeal as you learn about it from someone who has tried it and likes it, then consider whether their values are also yours; their judgments, similar to yours.

Why do I want to change? Is dislike of yourself the reason you want to change? Or is a positive belief that you can attain greater fulfillment your motive? Self-disgust sets up a vicious circle: "I am worthless, so I try to change myself. But because I think I'm worthless, I fail. Then I hate myself even more." Trying to change your sexual style is not a very useful way to work on self-confidence. Better to deal first with the heart of the problem before playing around with sexual alternatives in the vain hope that one of them will make you over.

Self-affirmation sets up an opposite kind of circle: "I may have some problems, but I appreciate who I am. I can change because I am worth the effort and the risk. When I fail, this tells me what I want to try next. When I succeed, this tells me I can make things even better." Feelings of adequacy tell you that you have some control over your own destiny: you can make changes that improve your life. Feelings of self-worth tell you that you deserve the satisfactions that change may bring. Self-affirming persons assert their power to be better than they are already. Of course, few people are madly in love with themselves as they are; indeed, people who seem that way may often be hiding a deep insecurity. Nevertheless, an underlying feeling of self-worth is necessary for any basic change in personal behavior. This is as true of the sexual as any area of our lives.

Are my goals realistic? Making changes in sexual style does not provide a fairy-tale ending, perpetual and explosive orgasms, "living happily ever after." Change does often provide some gain in and of itself. It offers variety. You really are making decisions and choosing values for yourself. Nevertheless, it is easy to be lured by sexy appearances, looking at other people and saying, "If only I were like that!" The woman beneath the flashy clothes and the man behind the suave manner are human, too; no doubt they have difficulties of their own. Since there is no perfect sexual style, there are bound to be some losses and some gains when you change. Both are important to consider. Are the rewards likely to outweigh the losses this change may entail?

Some goals might be quite realistic for someone else to consider but idle fancy in your particular situation. To decide that you do not want children when you already have three is at best frustrating and at worst child neglect. Rather than longing for the impossible, it is usually more satisfying to work on ways of getting more of what you want within your limitations. The tough-minded question you will want to ask yourself is, What are realistic goals *for me?*

Making Plans

The image of sexual change as a merry ride down a slippery slope must in the end be discarded for the simple reason that there is more than one decision to be made. You don't just decide on this slide or that one. You decide where you want to go and you plan how you are going to get there. There are many decisions to be made, some at the outset, some along the way. It is more like planning a backpacking trip through a beautiful mountain range. You make preparations. You draw up a plan. You want to enjoy yourself and minimize any danger of getting hurt or lost. Your plan is a flexible one because you have not been over the terrain before. A certain valley may appear too desolate, so you alter your route to go around it. The unexpected beauty of a sparkling stream may lead you to dawdle there a day or two. Never mind; your map keeps you heading where you want to go. Some people plan their trips for months ahead, having almost as much fun plotting the course as taking the trip.

You may be starting on this trip alone, expecting to meet your companions along the way. You can plan by yourself. But you may be going with someone else. In that case you may from the outset discuss with your partner where the two of you want to go and how you will get there. On the other hand, you may wish to do some thinking and planning alone before initiating discussion with your partner. You don't want to be overwhelmed by your partner's decided preferences while yours are still very tentative. In any case, one of the decisions you make is when, whether, and how you will negotiate your hopes and desires with those of a partner.

So you sit down at your desk alone or with company and begin sketching a plan. Here are four steps you can use in planning your sexual trip:

1. *Define your goals.* Where do you want to be, what is it precisely that you want to achieve? What will you look like as a sexual person when you have made your changes? Let your goals be specific, definable, even measurable. After all, if your goals are too vague, you won't even know when you get there. Let your goals be realistic, not dreams or fuzzy longings. Write your goals out. Goals written in black and white have a way of revealing themselves in living color. Put your goals in order of importance. What is most important? Which are the lesser goals required to reach your overall destination?

2. *Marshal your resources.* What can help you get where you want to be? What are the strengths, energies, and skills you already have that can help you modify your sexual style? What capacities do you have that need sharpening or developing to help you? What friends, books, counselors, or experts can provide assistance? Is your partner a resource who can and will experiment with you, hang in there when the going gets rough, and be honest in saying how he or she sees it? List your resources honestly and carefully. Both modesty and presumption are to be avoided.

3. *Predict the barriers.* What might stop you from achieving your goals? Consider the blocks and barriers that might arise along the way. Make a list of those that might create real difficulty. Check those barriers that are within you. These are the feelings of inertia, jealousy, guilt, shame, fear, and the like. Circle those barriers that are created by your environment or those around you. Your partner may be a barrier rather than a resource. Your job may be a problem. Again, be specific about these blocks. Look at them squarely; describe them as accurately as you can.

Now consider what you might do to remove or neutralize these barriers. Are there ways you could rearrange your work to interfere less with your life? Can you begin a dialogue with your partner about your differing desires? What steps can you take to reduce the blocks you feel within yourself? Which of the resources you catalogued can be applied directly to these barriers?

4. *Draw up a plan of action.* What is the first thing you would need to do to attain your first goal? What is the next? And the next? Break the whole process down into a series of intermediate steps. You may need to have a plan for developing your resources or a plan for dealing with your barriers before you launch on any grand plan for sexual revolution.

If the sexual changes you contemplate are a major trip, a well-structured plan covering months or even years may be useful. You can design a time line for yourself. Estimate how much time should be devoted to each of your intermediate steps. What do you need to do tomorrow? What will have to be done next week if the following week you are to go to the next step? You may want to make some contingency plans, alternate routes in case things do not go as planned. You may even mark some spots on the time line when you will decide whether to go on or turn back. The time line works best if you spread it out over several feet of brown paper so that you have plenty of room to write in the details. If you plan only a few sexual excursions, a time line will be much too elaborate. You can make do with simple checklists such as you might use to pack a picnic basket for a day at the beach. However, if you plan a major journey over new territory, the detailing of what you intend is almost indispensable.

Getting Under Way

Like everything else, sexual change begins at the beginning. You take that first step. Is it easier or more difficult than you expected? If it is easier, great! If it is more difficult, should it be broken down into smaller steps? Do you need to handle unexpected difficulties? Is the process more or less enjoyable than you imagined?

Occasional reevaluation of your plan is an essential part of the change process. Your plan of action is a tool to help you achieve what you wish. It is not an ideal that you must live up to, not a test of your self-worth. If unexpected barriers arise or you fail to overcome some block, modify your plan or your time line. Do you need to spend longer on a given problem or change your goal? Is there another way to achieve the same goal or another way to surmount the barrier? Don't keep butting your head, or some other part of your anatomy, against a wall. There's probably a way around it.

Determination to change is important. A person who does not try is not likely to realize cherished goals. Yet trying hard is not the secret of change, certainly not in things sexual. In fact trying too hard is self-defeating. Trying to have an orgasm, trying to have an erection, trying to respond to a given caress—in each case, effort produces failure. But neither does one have an orgasm by avoiding all genital manipulation. Effort pays off primarily in the way you organize your life so that sexual enjoyment can happen. To pursue a certain sexual style may require effort and planning in order to arrange your life so that your sexual existence can take the shape you wish it to have. But when it comes to sexual response and love-making itself, lay off the effort and let it happen.

In charting a course of action you can overwhelm yourself with all the barriers that *might* block your path. You can conjure up so many difficulties that you give up the plan before it really gets under way. There is a fine line between being realistic about dangers and talking yourself out of ever taking action. Barriers can appear as exciting challenges or impassable roadblocks. How do yours appear? Are you willing to tackle them in order to achieve the changes you desire?

It is, of course, not necessary to feel bad if you later discover that you no longer wish to change. The new way may be doing violence to you or your partner. The gains may not be compensating for the losses. If this happens and you decide to turn away from the goals you set, you can understand your attempt as a clarification exercise. You can return to your former style with greater certainty that it is the one for you.

On the other hand, if you continue to move step by step toward your goals, an occasional self-evaluation will show your progress and let you give yourself a pat on the back. You can see how far you have come and what you have accomplished. Progress may be slow. You may decide to move even slower. As in sex, so in sexual style—speed is no virtue. Yet over time, as you see the change taking place, you will have a deep sense of satisfaction in your achievement.

It would be presumptuous of us to tell you, sight unseen, how to deal with the special set of problems or barriers you might encounter. You are a unique person. You have your own foibles and your own special gifts. It would be quackery to prescribe your course of action. What we have been exploring is not treatment but ways of assuming responsibility for your actions and the choices you make. This is a method, a structure, by which you can chart a course for yourself. In sex you do not put yourself into the hands of a pilot and navigator, choosing only your destination, leaving the route up to them. Instead, you choose not only the journey's destination but the method of travel and the terrain you traverse.

A Pocket Guide to Choosing Values

As we conclude this search through sexual values, we have two pleasant concerns to complete. First, we shall summarize the method we have been using throughout the book so that you may apply it to issues of special concern to you, ones we have not addressed. This can be a little pocket guide to choosing your sexual values. Second, we want to toast your achievement in staying with what must frequently have been, in spite of all enjoyment, a difficult and threatening enterprise.

Eight steps make up this method of choosing sexual values:

1. *You increase your awareness of what is important to you.* What do you prize and what do you cherish? You look at what you are doing sexually and seek to isolate what it is that you really want. You search your whole being for clues to what matters most. This is done in both thought and feeling, with your mind and with your emotions.

2. *You line up all the options.* You separate them one from the other so that you will know what your choices actually are. You compare the way you have been living or hope to live sexually with other available options. You consider even those choices which at first glance seem quite unacceptable. Thus, the choices you finally make are a thoughtful selection made on the basis of your courageous willingness to look at all the alternatives.

3. *You choose your method of choosing sexual values.* You may use one method exclusively, such as a consideration of consequences, or you may use more than one method in some combination. You may go at every sexual question with the same method, or you may use different methods or different kinds of questions, say, taste for the way you enjoy genital contact, and authority for whom you have genital contact with. You are clear about your own way of choosing.

4. *You select your "live options."* Now you are checking out your freedom to choose the options that are most appealing to you. You locate the barriers that might make a choice difficult or impossible. You examine the limitations on your sexual life, limitations within you and around you. You discard those options which appear to be unrealistic dreams; you look for those with a good chance of realization.

5. *You apply your method of choosing to the options you are now considering.* If you are choosing on the basis of consequences, you then analyze the positive and negative results likely for each of the alternatives you are seriously weighing. If you are using the method of universalizing reason, you will ponder whether or not you are willing to have other people act the way you are considering. Whatever method is yours, you apply it directly to the available options.

6. *You test out your options in imagination.* You try a fantasy, design a strategy, or give yourself a quiz. You may copy or adapt some of the procedures suggested in this book. Or you use your own creativity to become aware of what it would be like to act out a sexual style you are contemplating. You use mental and emotional images to picture the styles you like best.

7. *You test out your options in actions.* You give your sexual choices a very self-conscious action test. If you are considering something new, you

try it out, not impulsively or blindly, but carefully and intentionally, testing in action whether this new way feels right in reality, works for you in practice, actually brings out what you intended.

8. *You find the options that endure over time.* You may change your values from time to time, but they do not jump around beneath you like the floor of a carnival fun house. When you have tried out a new option in action only once or twice, that is not yet a value. When you act on the basis of a given value with some consistency and persistence, that becomes your sexual style.

If you go through these steps with any sexual issue that has been confusing, you will become clearer about your sexual values. You have then considered the important alternatives; you have located the values that you feel most deeply and believe most earnestly; you have confirmed these by the consistency of your action. When that has taken place, you have your own sexual style. It is yours. Really yours! You are as sure as it is humanly possible to be sure that you are making the right sexual choices for you.

That is the method. Simple, but not easy. It takes work and guts. Chances are you are willing to pay that price. From now on, you can have the fun of designing your own games in a way that will enable you to live what Socrates called "the examined life." Or as Hermann Hesse describes it, "Each man's life represents a road toward himself, an attempt at such a road, the intimation of a path. No man has ever been entirely and completely himself. Yet each one strives to become that—one in an awkward, the other in a more intelligent way, each as best he can. . . . But each of us—experiments of the depths—strives toward his own destiny."[1]

Bon Voyage!

So, a toast to us all! We have come this far together. If you have struggled and striven to get through all the games and questions we have thrown at you, you are the kind of person who, we believe, makes an unloving world more loving. We are frequently asked, "How can you have such an optimistic view of human nature? You expect so much of people." If it occurred to you to ask that question as you made your way through these pages, you probably asked it in relation to other people. You are not really surprised that we believe in you, are you?

Actually, the fact is that our view of human nature is anything but rosy. This is indeed a world of tragedy. There is inhumanity and cruelty both in the intercourse of groups and nations and in the intimacy of home and bed. The cruelty seems most tragic where we least expect it. No, we are not optimistic. Rather, we believe there is a narrow margin of choice over which we are each masters. What we do with this meager measure of freedom is the stuff of which the human future is formed. It is no counsel of perfection to suggest that the quality of human decency will be better served if we concern ourselves with the quality of love that feeds our lives. One of the wonderful faces of love is sexual, sensual love. Our most certain hope is that the lure of a more satisfying sexual love will be a motivation in your pursuit of a more fully human destiny.

Therefore, the encouragement we offer in parting is not that you can do everything you wish nor that your search for sexual integrity will be easy. Rather, it is that you, with all your frailties, are worth believing in. Your willingness to risk, to try new possibilities, to give up useless habits, to surrender increasingly to what you really love—these are marks of your personal worth.

That statement has both the sound of hope and a ring of uncertainty. No one can tell you to believe in yourself. Unless you do already, you cannot hear it from anyone else. However, you have chosen to keep responsibility for your sexual self firmly in your own hands. For you, your self-esteem comes from the little steps by which you are able to bring your life into more ordered relationship to your desires and convictions.

You are a "person on the way," *homo viator*. It is very ancient wisdom that suggests that the essence of being human is thinking toward the future, living today in the light of tomorrow. Whatever wilderness you may encounter on the way, may your pilgrimage be filled with joy. *Bon voyage!*

Epilogue:
A Sexual Creed

The pursuit of sexual values we have followed in this book is based on the desire to facilitate your search for personal values, not on a desire to influence you to agree with us. We have tried to be objective—but perfect objectivity is impossible. In order to minimize the effect of our own bias, we append this statement of our own sexual beliefs.

We hope that this will free you further from any influence of our own views. We do believe deeply in our own understanding of the sexual person. We have some basic convictions about appropriate ways to act out our sexual natures, but we do not claim for these beliefs any special authority. We only hope that, as the views of any serious seeker, they might be considered earnestly. We offer these affirmations as a final contribution to the dialogue, suggesting that you bounce your own views off the backboard of these ideas, to see where and with what intensity you may agree or disagree with us.

We also make this statement of our sexual creed as an invitation to you to write your own creed. From the beginning we have admitted that a book is a less than satisfactory way of engaging in a dialogue over something as deeply personal as sex. We should rather talk it over with you around the fireplace. We are all conscious that finally we have made inadequate connections between your life of feeling and imagination and our own. We therefore have suggested that you write your own sexual autobiography, that you go back over the rich detail of your own sexual story and isolate the critical events that have shaped your attitudes and feelings, your ideas and your values. We have suggested the usefulness of complete privacy in writing your story, putting the emphasis on your own awareness of your history, without any need to be concerned with the response of other persons.

We now suggest that you consider writing a sexual creed, that you seek to formulate as clearly as possible your own most fundamental beliefs about sex. We suggest that you consider the major options available and place yourself somewhere in relation to them. This does not mean, of course, that your faith will be frozen today at the points where you put yourself. There is no need to stop changing, to quit growing. Rather, let it be a milestone. This is who I am today. There are continuities with my history, and there will be consistency with my future, but I am not entirely bound by the past and neither do I have to remain exactly as I am. However, I do place myself somewhere. I am not a mish-mash of beliefs and feelings. I am somebody. I am sexual. I have sexual values. They are a fundamental part of who I am.

Unlike the sexual autobiography, with the suggestion of privacy, we suggest that if you have a partner, you make the writing of your sexual creed a joint endeavor. If you are in relationship with another person sexually, you may find it an exercise in communication to sort out your sexual values together. That may be a bit frightening. It can also be deeply satisfying.

Here is our statement of sexual values:

We believe in a sexual style that makes sex an integral part of the entire range of human values. Sex is not simply a biological function, separable from other human concerns. When separated from the other values that make existence fulfilling, it becomes an obsession and a slavery. Sex can infuse all relationships with its power and creativity, not just those usually thought of as sexual. There is an erotic dimension to friendship, to family relationships, to intellectual and vocational endeavors. When this is repressed, the result is dishonesty and potential disaster. Sex is not synonymous with orgasm.

We believe in expressive sex. We are capable of mind-blowing, body-invigorating, spiritually ecstatic sexual experience. This is not a goal to be attained. It is rather a natural result of our humanness when we stop putting roadblocks in the way. This includes a wide range of kinds and intensities of erotic experience. Often it is orgasmic in character, a final and sudden, sometimes repetitive, explosion of feeling and satisfaction. At other times it is soft and subtle, a prolonged sensual encounter in which each nuance is fondled in a harmony of craving and satiation. To be sexually expressive is to be emotionally expressive. To be in touch with another is to be in touch with oneself. To be in touch with oneself is to be in touch with another.

We believe in touch. We believe touching each other is important in our relationship. We believe touching other persons besides each other is important in our relationship. We find extraordinary enjoyment in massage. The miracle of skin and form, muscle and bone, seeing, hearing, smelling, touching—these we celebrate in the ritual of contact.

We believe in relational sex. There may be value in incidental sexual contacts under certain circumstances, but we affirm the greater and more enduring joy of two human beings entering deeply into each other's existence. No fleeting contact can possibly rival the depth and wonder of this experience. The quaint phrase of the King James Bible describes sexual intercourse as "knowledge." "And Adam knew Eve." To say, "I love you," when I know who you are, the beauty and the blemishes, is to enter the realm of understanding. To have that expressed in the intermingling of bodies is to enter into joy. There are special dangers in relational sex, the dangers of jealousy and possessiveness, even of dullness and boredom, but these are the products of anxieties and attitudes that will spoil any sexual style. We find the satisfactions of a deep relationship provide the security with which our anxieties are often relieved.

We believe in sexual communication. This includes sex as a form of communication, a way of saying what cannot be said, of feeling together what cannot otherwise be felt. This also includes communication about sex. We are not mind readers, capable of immediately comprehending the other's nature and needs. We believe in nonverbal communication, ways by which our very bodies, even in spite of our intentions, say what wants to be said. But we also believe in verbal communication, in reducing the guesswork. We believe in making feeling statements, in each of us taking responsibility for his or her own feelings. We believe in asking questions, in resolving ambiguities, in testing out hunches. We believe in talk; we believe in talk about sex.

We believe in independence. Each is his or her own person. A relationship is not made good by turning over one's own destiny to another. Sex is not made good simply by giving the partner what is wanted. We each must bring a real person to the sexual encounter, to the relationship. We each have our own needs, our own desires, our own ways of being "turned on." To deny these is to deny each other the gift of our presence.

We believe in interdependence. Sex is finally a radical interdependence. We do surrender to each other. Our lives and our bodies are mutually interdependent. Total independence is a myth and a prison of loneliness.

But complete dependence always seems to be one-sided; one person is dependent on the other. Dependence and interdependence are mutually exclusive. To be capable of surrender is to be capable of love. Without that surrender orgasm does not take place. To enter ecstasy requires that we "let go."

We believe in freedom with commitment. Commitment need not require giving over one's autonomy. The traditional marriage vows seem almost to give possession of the self over to the spouse, especially the wife over to the husband. This we resist. Absolute freedom, of course, exists only in the minds of dreamers. To be free at all requires a structure within which freedom functions. We believe in negotiated commitment, partners communicating long and hard to develop mutual expectations satisfying to those concerned. We believe in renegotiated commitment, in the realization that we cannot know precisely and for certain how we will feel in a year or a decade.

We believe in trust. This is what makes possible holding freedom and commitment together. If each trusts the other, you do not have to have an ironclad, legally enforceable commitment that you imagine will guarantee that you will always behave toward your partner as you now promise. With trust the commitment is believable and viable. Without trust the commitment is worthless. With trust each can allow the other freedom; without it you cannot even allow yourself freedom. With the values of freedom, commitment, and trust operating between us, we no longer need concern ourselves with the petty details of who is fooling around with whom, when, where, or how. We have the incredible luxury of enjoying each other, of enjoying ourselves with each other, of enjoying the world together.

We believe in equality. Specifically, we believe in equality between the sexes, in the equality between the two of us. It sometimes feels rather discouraging when the whole world seems set up to require that we treat each other differently. It is even more discouraging when we discover again and again how much we still act inequitably when there is no one to blame but ourselves. In spite of it all, we do believe that we can grow in equality, that we need not exploit each other, that old stereotypes can be overcome. We believe this because we have discovered how wonderful it is when we meet each other as unique persons. There are creative possibilities that go beyond traditional roles and expectations. There are differences between us as male and female, but they are only a part of the differences between us as persons. The so-called female characteristics of passivity, gentleness, sensitivity, and subordination do not conform to our experience. The so-called male characteristics of aggressiveness, initiative, strength, and dispassion are equally artificial. We commit ourselves to that freedom which chooses flexibly, according to time and circumstance, from the rich variety of behavior available in the interest of human values that transcend gender.

We believe in all these values as possibilities we may allow to happen. They are not norms we must live up to. It is disastrous in sex to struggle to live up to any standard of performance, no matter how great and wonderful. We can no more try to love someone than we can try to have an orgasm. These are things that must be allowed to happen, more related to spontaneity than to intention. We can pick and choose values intellectually forever, and it will make no real difference until we become sensitive to our own feelings and desires, learning to act out of them in relation to thoughtful judgments. It does not matter whether the standards we are trying to conform to are the traditional ones that hold us within a narrow range of behavior and styles of sex or whether the standard is a "liberation" that requires that we try everything and enjoy anything.

We believe in consent. Sex cannot be forced on any partner without distressing results. This applies in obvious ways to physical coercion; it applies also to styles of seduction that mislead, so that the respondent is robbed of choice. It applies especially to long-term intimate relationships, including marriage, in which the atmosphere may be coercive and rob one or both partners of real choice. We deeply disbelieve in sexual manipulation. Consent must be respected, not only sensitively and perceptively in allowing the partner freedom, but even in oneself. You must let yourself be, allow yourself freedom, act only when you give your true consent.

We believe in the privacy of sex. This means that most of what people do sexually is their own business and no one else's. This is a great change over traditional views, which were based on the assumption that the community had a large stake in sexual behavior. We believe that there are few sexual issues in which the public has any stake. As long as people carry on their sexual activities in private and with the consent of all who are affected by these activities, there is little reason for laws or even social sanctions to govern behavior. Much behavior that was one called morally wrong or psychologically deviant need no longer be so labeled. People can exploit one another in any style of sexual behavior. Heterosexual intercourse in the "usual way" is no guarantee that the partners will not misuse one another. Any act can be wrong and deviant when it emanates from a dynamic that is destructive for either one of us.

We believe in the search for a morality that will replace the ethics of procreation with sexual styles that are responsible to the human ecosystem. We believe that wanton increase in population and consumption promises disaster for the human race. Sex becomes a matter of public concern whenever children are involved. We do not imply compulsory contraception, sterilization, or abortion. We do imply resistance to social values that support the begetting of children as an automatic ideal. We do intend the removal of impediments and the providing of public assistance to persons who wish to control conception. We do intend to reject the authority of religious perspectives that sanction values outmoded under contemporary ecological circumstances.

We believe that the sanctity of human life endorses the value of sex for its own sake. Sex is not only a means to other values such as intimacy and security, family or children. It is an amazing joy in and of itself. We celebrate sex as a quality of experience which transcends the pettiness of daily existence!

Notes

■──■

Introduction: Is There a Better Way?

1.   This approach to values is based upon the pioneering work of Louis Raths, Harmin Merril, and Sidney Simon, *Values and Teaching* (Columbus, Ohio: Charles E. Merrill, 1966). Other works of Simon and Merril, as well as those of Leland W. Howe, Howard Kirschenbaum, and Eleanor Morrison, have influenced our approach. It will be clear to anyone acquainted with this literature that we have departed from the usual values-clarification approach in a number of ways. We have omitted "choosing after consideration of consequences" as a *necessary* part of the valuing process. There are criteria other than consequences upon which to base the consideration of alternatives, as the history of ethics and the current inquiry demonstrate. We invite readers not only to consider consequences but also to evaluate options on the basis of other criteria as well. See Chapter 10 in which we have attempted to float the clarification process free from pragmatism by providing ways of evaluating value alternatives.

3.   Getting In Deep

1.   William H. Masters and Virginia E. Johnson, in *Sexuality and Human Values*, ed. Mary S. Calderone (New York: Association Press, 1974), p. 88.

2.   W. Dennis, "Causes of Retardation among Institutional Children: Iran," *Journal of Genetic Psychology* 96 (1960): 46–60.

4.   Solo Sex

1.   As recently as 1973, one study showed that 22 percent of all medical students believed that masturbation is a contributory factor in mental illness. See Harold I. Lief, "Obstacles to the Ideal and Complete Sex Education of Medical Student and Physician," in *Contemporary Sexual Behavior: Critical Issues in the 70's*, ed. Joseph Zubin and John Money (Baltimore: Johns Hopkins University Press, 1973), p. 447.

2.   Paul Abramson, "The Relationship of Frequency of Masturbation to Several Aspects of Personality and Behavior," in *Perspectives on Human*

Sexuality, ed. Nathaniel N. Wagner (New York: Behavioral Publications, 1974).

5. Just Sex, Please: The Casual Style

1. Helen Singer Kaplan, *The Illustrated Manual of Sex Therapy* (New York: Quadrangle, 1975), p. 178.

2. William H. Masters and Virginia E. Johnson, in association with Robert J. Levin, *The Pleasure Bond* (New York: Bantam Books, 1976), p. 189.

6. Sex with Love: The Relational Style

1. Kaplan, *Illustrated Manual of Sex Therapy*, p. 178.

2. For example, ibid.

3. For example, C. A. Tripp, *The Homosexual Matrix* (New York: McGraw-Hill, 1975).

7. Sex with Love . . . and Someone on the Side: The Supplemented Style

1. In his study *Sexual Behavior in the 1970's* (Chicago: Playboy Press, 1974), p. 257, Morton Hunt estimates that nearly half of all married males have had extramarital sex. His estimates for married females are much lower. However, in a *Redbook* magazine survey (to which 100,000 women replied), although only 29 percent overall said they had had extramarital sex, fully 53 percent of wives in the thirty-five to thirty-nine age bracket who are employed full-time admitted extramarital sex. This led the authors to surmise that as more and more women join the work force, their extramarital behavior will more closely approximate men's. The fact that this is a self-selecting sample would not necessarily affect this projection. Carol Tavris and Susan Sadd, *The Redbook Report on Female Sexuality* (New York: Dell, 1978).

2. Estimates of mate swapping range from 1 percent in Gilbert Bartell's study *Group Sex* (New York: New American Library, 1974), to 5 percent in a 1969 survey in *Psychology Today*, February 1975, p. 55. Other estimates in Hunt, *Sexual Behavior in the 1970's*, and in James R. Smith and Lynn G. Smith, eds., *Beyond Monogamy: Recent Studies of Sexual Alternatives in Marriage* (Baltimore: Johns Hopkins University Press, 1974), fall somewhere between these extremes. The figures on group marriage are even smaller. Joan and Larry Constantine for their study of group marriage followed over two hundred leads. They found thirty-one multilateral marriages and got sixteen groups to participate in their study. However, eleven of these dissolved before the study was completed (Larry Constantine and Joan Constantine, "Sexual Aspects of Multi-

lateral Relations," in *Beyond Monogamy*, ed. Smith and Smith). Thus, group marriages available for research have been not only rare but also unstable.

3. John Cuber, "Adultery: Reality versus Stereotype," in *Human Sexuality: Contemporary Perspectives*, ed. Eleanor S. Morrison and Vera Borosage (Palo Alto, Calif.: National Press Books, 1973), p. 164.

8. Forsaking All Others: The Total Style

1. John Cuber and Peggy Haroff, *Sex and the Significant Americans* (New York: Appleton-Century, 1965). The total style is one among five marital styles that these two researchers isolated in this study. Anyone interested in marriage styles in general, not just in sexual styles, might be interested in reading this book.

9. Kids: The Procreative Style

1. Howard J. Clinebell and Charlotte H. Clinebell, *The Intimate Marriage* (New York: Harper & Row, 1970), pp. 69, 205.

2. This is a study of 2,164 adults done at the University of Michigan Institute of Social Research by Angus Campbell et al., published as *The Quality of American Life: Perceptions, Evaluations and Satisfactions*, by Angus Campbell (New York: Russell Sage Foundation, 1976). A popular report is to be found in "The American Way of Mating" by William Rogers and Angus Campbell, *Psychology Today* 8, no. 12 (May 1975): 37–43.

3. In Chapter 6 of *Solomon's Sword: Clarifying Values in the Church* (Nashville, Tenn.: Abingdon Press, 1977) we have developed a series of values-clarification exercises on abortion as a religious issue.

10. Choosing a Way to Choose

1. A variety of these religious perspectives, ranging from conservative to radical, are listed and annotated in the Bibliography. In addition, the diversity may be further explored in the statements of different denominations. These vary from the traditional Roman Catholic position, represented by the encyclical *Humanae Vitae* (1968) of Pope Paul VI, to a current official study document of the United Church of Christ, *Human Sexuality: A Preliminary Study* (New York: United Church Press, 1977).

11. Pigeonholes

1. The first and seventh statements are false. Through loneliness, older heterosexual men may seek affection from males if there are no available hetero-

sexual partners. Prostate surgery does not always produce impotency, depending on the character of the surgery as well as on psychological factors. These statements are based on William H. Masters and Virginia E. Johnson, *Human Sexual Response* (Boston: Little, Brown, 1966), Chapters 15 and 16; and on James Leslie McCary, *Sexual Myths and Fallacies* (New York: Schocken Books, 1973).

2.   Masters and Johnson, *Human Sexual Response*, pp. 262, 240ff.

3.   Ibid., and McCary, *Sexual Myths and Fallacies*.

12.   Communicating Your Sexual Style

1.   Robert Levin and Amy Levin, "Sexual Pleasure: The Surprising Preferences of 100,000 Women," *Redbook*, September 1975. Reprint.

2.   R. D. Laing, *Knots* (New York: Pantheon Books, 1970), p. 56.

3.   R. D. Laing, H. Phillipson, and A. R. Lee, *Interpersonal Perception* (New York: Harper & Row, Perennial Library, 1972).

14.   Charting Change

1.   Hermann Hesse, *Demian* (New York: Harper & Row, 1965), prologue.

Bibliography

∎──∎

This Bibliography is highly selective. We have included only those books that we have found particularly useful or that might be of interest or help to the reader in pursuing matters not dealt with comprehensively here. More extensive bibliographies can be found in the scholarly books on this list. Since the literature on sexuality is expanding rapidly, current publication lists should also be consulted.

Physiology, Sexual Response, and Sociological Research

Boston Women's Health Book Collective. *Our Bodies, Ourselves: A Book By and For Women*, revised edition. New York: Simon & Schuster, 1976.

Explains female physiology and all aspects of reproduction and childbirth. Offers support to women seeking alternative life-styles and better health care.

Brecher, Edward M. *The Sex Researchers*. New York: Signet, 1971.

A popular account of sex research from Havelock Ellis to Masters and Johnson. Covers important findings of the sex researchers in nontechnical language.

Cuber, John, and Haroff, Peggy. *Sex and the Significant Americans*. New York: Appleton-Century, 1965.

A study of 437 upper-middle-class, successful Americans, who reveal in in-depth interviews a number of styles that marriage can take. Verbatim excerpts often insightful and illustrate how different values make different styles appropriate for different people.

Diagram Group. *Man's Body: An Owner's Manual*. New York: Paddington Press, 1976.

Focus is on the physiology, health problems, and care of the male body. Discussion of male sexuality follows this clinical vein.

Hunt, Morton. *The Affair*. New York: Signet, 1973.

Ninety-one in-depth interviews with people currently or previously involved in extramarital sex provide the basis for describing and theorizing about the affair. Excerpts from the interviews add flavor and insight.

Hunt, Morton. *Sexual Behavior in the 1970's*. Chicago: Playboy Press, 1974.

Report of a survey undertaken to update some of the Kinsey research—to see who is doing what in the seventies. Not as extensive as Kinsey, but useful both for the comparisons provided and for more recent data.

Masters, William H., and Johnson, Virginia E. *Human Sexual Response*. Boston: Little, Brown, 1966.

The standard work on how the sexual response works in males and females, in the young and aging—written in technical language.

McCary, James Leslie. *Human Sexuality*, second edition. New York: D. Van Nostrand Reinhold, 1973; also paperback brief edition, D. Van Nostrand, 1973.

A useful basic text on human sexuality. Discusses physiology, sexual function and dysfunction, and sexual behavior patterns, among other aspects of sexuality.

Neubeck, Gerhard, ed. *Extra-Marital Relations*. Englewood Cliffs, N.J.: Prentice-Hall, 1969.

A collection of studies and essays on extramarital sex. Attitudes toward extramarital sex here and abroad are explored, as well as some research on the effect of outside sex on marriage.

Sadock, Benjamin J.; Kaplan, Harold I.; and Freedman, Alfred M., eds. *The Sexual Experience*. Baltimore: Williams & Wilkins, 1976.

With chapters written by both medical doctors and other authorities, this book provides a thorough overview of almost all aspects of sexual experience. Historical, developmental, biological, functional, and social aspects of sexuality are covered.

Sex Differences

Lee, Patrick C., and Steward, Robert Sussman, eds. *Sex Differences*. New York: Urizen Books, 1976.

A collection of writings from people who have had significant influence on the views of the sexes current in this century. Explores sex differences from the psychoanalytic, anthropological, sociological, bio-ethological, and psychological dimensions.

Maccoby, Eleanor Emmons, and Jacklin, Carol Nagy. *The Psychology of Sex Differences*. Stanford, Calif.: Stanford University Press, 1974.

A sequel to an earlier volume, it reports on research published since 1966 on how the sexes do and do not differ. Covers vast amounts of research and has an extensive annotated bibliography. Along with its predecessor, the standard work on sex differentiation development.

Money, John, and Ehrhardt, Anke A. *Man & Woman, Boy & Girl: Differentia-tion and Dimorphism of Gender Identity*. Baltimore: Johns Hopkins University Press, 1972.

A fascinating, but somewhat technical, description of twenty years of research into gender identity at Johns Hopkins University. Covers the results of research on sex hormones, hermaphroditism, and other sex defects in discussing the nature versus nurture controversy and the development of sexual identity.

Sex Therapy

Belliveau, Fred, and Richter, Lin. *Understanding Human Sexual Inadequacy*. New York: Bantam Books, 1970.

A popular account of Masters and Johnson's research and therapeutic approach, using nontechnical, easily understood language.

Hartman, William E., and Fithian, Marilyn A. *Treatment of Sexual Dysfunction: A Bio-Psycho-Social Approach*. New York: Jason Aronson, 1974.

An explicit account of the authors' dual sex team therapy approach, it includes sample sex history questionnaires and various treatment procedures.

Kaplan, Helen Singer. *The Illustrated Manual of Sex Therapy*. New York: Quadrangle, 1975.

A supplement to her general text on sex therapy, this book is for both therapists and patients. It contains pictures illustrating techniques useful for treating six major dysfunctions.

Kaplan, Helen Singer. *The New Sex Therapy: Active Treatment of Sexual Dysfunctions*. New York: Quadrangle, 1974.

Describes in detail the author's approach to sex therapy, which combines elements of both Masters and Johnson's and psychoanalytic treatment procedures.

Masters, William H., and Johnson, Virginia E. *Human Sexual Inadequacy*. Boston: Little, Brown, 1970.

The pioneering work on human sexual dysfunction and the dual sex team therapy approach that these two authors developed. Quite technical language used.

Essays and "Point of View" Books

Barbach, Lonnie Garfield. *For Yourself*. Garden City, N.Y.: Anchor Books, 1976.

Written by a woman for women who wish to enhance or enrich their appreciation of themselves as sexual beings. Specific exercises provided.

Clinebell, Howard J., and Clinebell, Charlotte H. *The Intimate Marriage*. New York: Harper & Row, 1970.

Written by a couple involved in pastoral and marriage counseling, this book argues for, and offers help for, achieving a total marriage style.

Comfort, Alex, ed. *The Joy of Sex*. New York: Crown, 1972.

Offers a wealth of ideas for people who wish to improve or put variety into their lovemaking. Nicely illustrated. Some help is offered for sexual problems, but the book's main strength lies in its material to make good sex better.

Francoeur, Robert T., and Francoeur, Anna K., eds. *The Future of Sexual Relations*. Englewood Cliffs, N.J.: Prentice-Hall, 1974.

A group of essays exploring a variety of possibilities emerging in a changing sexual climate. Essayists include prominent figures in sexology, anthropology, theology, and so on.

Gordon, Sol, and Libby, Roger W., eds. *Sexuality Today—and Tomorrow*. Belmont, Calif.: Duxbury Press, 1976.

A collection of articles and essays that look at sexual behavior today, the political, social, and personal issues involved, and make some predictions about and pleas for appropriate sexual behavior in the future.

Libby, Roger W., and Whitehurst, Robert N., eds. *Renovating Marriage*. Danville, Calif.: Consensus Publishers, 1973.

A collection of articles and essays that report on research and explore sexual styles that are alternatives to traditional monogamous marriage. A wide variety of alternative styles and possibilities for the future is considered.

Masters, William H., and Johnson, Virginia E., in association with Robert J. Levin. *The Pleasure Bond*. New York: Bantam Books, 1976.

Reports on five symposiums held by Masters and Johnson as part of an effort to determine what is essential to the achievement of sexual pleasure. The issues they isolate as being central are then further discussed.

Mazur, Ronald. *The New Intimacy: Open-Ended Marriage and Alternative Life-Styles*. Boston: Beacon Press, 1973.

Written by a Unitarian-Universalist minister and sex educator, this book argues for more flexibility for all in choosing sexual styles and for the open-marriage style in particular.

Morrison, Eleanor, and Borosage, Vera, eds. *Human Sexuality: Contemporary Perspectives*, second edition. Palo Alto, Calif.: National Press Books, 1977.

One of the few collections of articles and essays that offers a range of viewpoints on various aspects of sexual behavior—from very traditional to very nontraditional.

O'Neill, Nena, and O'Neill, George. *Open Marriage: A New Life-Style for Couples.* New York: Avon Books, 1972.

Written by a husband and wife who argue forcefully for a style of marriage in which openness and freedom are made priorities of the relationship.

Smith, James R., and Smith, Lynn G., eds. *Beyond Monogamy: Recent Studies of Sexual Alternatives in Marriage.* Baltimore: Johns Hopkins University Press, 1974.

A collection of essays and studies on styles of sexual behavior to replace traditional monogamous marriage; in particular it concentrates on research into and interpretation of mate swapping, group marriage, and other forms of comarital sex.

Values, Religion, and Sexuality

Bailey, D. Sherwin. *Sexual Relations in Christian Thought.* New York: Harper, 1959.

One among several important and carefully researched books by this author on this subject. Somewhat dated by subsequent biblical studies, but generally definitive.

Borowitz, Eugene B. *Choosing a Sex Ethic: A Jewish Inquiry.* New York: Schocken Books, 1970.

A rabbi examines optional ethical views for young people and concludes with his own perspective.

Calderone, Mary S., ed. *Sexuality and Human Values.* New York: Association Press, 1974.

Based on a conference on religion and sexuality, a series of well-known experts discuss the role of religious and human values in sexual functioning and behavior. Raises many provocative issues in challenging churches to provide more adequate responses to human sexuality.

Callahan, Daniel. *Abortion: Law, Choice and Morality.* New York: Macmillan, 1970.

A definitive study of the issues surrounding abortion, with a broad base of information and ethical reflection. A public document originating in the Hastings Institute.

Friends Home Service Committee. *Toward a Quaker View of Sex.* London: Friends House, 1963.

A pioneering liberal view of sexuality based not on rules but on Christian humanistic concern with relationships and persons. The document represents the views of the committee who prepared it and not the views of the Society of Friends as such.

Kennedy, Eugene. *What a Modern Catholic Believes about Sex*. Chicago: Thomas More, 1975.

A moderate Catholic perspective on sexual values.

Kosnik, Anthony, et al. *Human Sexuality: New Directions in American Catholic Thought*. New York: Paulist Press, 1977.

Commissioned by the prestigious Catholic Theological Society of America, this book is a milestone of progressive Catholic thought.

Nelson, James B. *Embodiment: An Approach to Sexuality and Christian Theology*. Minneapolis: Augsburg, 1978.

A comprehensive study of the Christian implications of human sexuality, written by someone well versed in the theological, sociological, and psychological literature of sexuality. Insightful and thought provoking.

Pittenger, W. Norman. *Love and Control in Sexuality*. Philadelphia: United Church Press, 1974.

A process theologian examines questions of sexual ethics in this and other highly readable books.

Valente, M. F. *Sex: The Radical View of a Catholic Theologian*. New York: Bruce Books, 1970.

Part of a new development in Catholic thought that rejects the traditional points of view.

Wynn, John C., ed. *Sexual Ethics and Christian Responsibility—Some Divergent Views*. New York: Association Press, 1970.

A group of essays by prominent theologians, expressing a wide range of positions from liberal to conservative toward changes in sexual morality.

Homosexuality

Gearhart, Sally, and Johnson, William R., eds. *Loving Women/Loving Men: Gay Liberation and the Church*. San Francisco: Glide Publications, 1974.

A gay man and a gay woman ask for more openness in the church for homosexual life-styles.

McNeill, John J. *The Church and the Homosexual*. Kansas City: Sheed, Andrews and McMeel, 1976.

The first public affirmation that homosexuality can be an acceptable life-style from the Catholic perspective, by a Roman Catholic priest.

Nomadic Sisters. *Loving Women*. Sonora, Calif.: The Nomadic Sisters, 1975.

A self-help book for women who wish to improve or enrich their same-sex erotic styles. Nicely illustrated with line drawings.

Other Sources

These are but a few of the national sources from which further guidance might be obtained or from whom lists of local sources of professional help might be available.

American Association of Marriage and Family Counselors
225 Yale Avenue
Claremont, Calif. 91711

Supplies lists of certified marriage counselors.

American Association of Sex Educators, Counselors and Therapists (AASECT)
5010 Wisconsin Avenue, N.W.
Suite 304
Washington, D.C. 20016

Supplies lists of AASECT certified sex educators, counselors, and therapists.

Minnesota Couples Communication Course
Interpersonal Communication Programs, Inc.
300 Clifton Avenue at The Carriage House
Minneapolis, Minn. 55403

Supplies books outlining their communication course and lists of leaders trained in their method.

Planned Parenthood—Federation of America
810 Seventh Avenue
New York, N.Y. 10019

Supplies both publications and information about local Planned Parenthood offices dealing with contraception, abortion, and sex education.

Sex Information and Education Council of the United States (SIECUS)
84 Fifth Avenue
New York, N.Y. 10011

A nonprofit organization providing education and information on a wide variety of sexual matters.

Marriage Encounter
sponsored by many churches—check locally

Originally started by a Roman Catholic priest, many churches now sponsor these workshops, which focus on enriching the marriage relationship, sexually and otherwise.